What people ar

Wo

Sure-footed, Rachel S Roberts guides us through European myth, to meet our misunderstood cousins. You will dive deep to find your wild feminine nature – and with her guidance, you will courageously leap out to greet your human pack with a howl!
Rachel O'Leary, author of *The Swan-Bone Flute*

Wolf, by Rachel Roberts, is a book for anyone who wants to learn about the lives, myths, legends, and stories of these enigmatic and inspiring creatures, then use that knowledge for personal development and spiritual empowerment. She offers an in-depth look at how wolves behave in their natural habitat, how humans have interacted with them over millennia, how they have been woven into mythology, and how they have come to symbolise things we fear but also our own wild nature. Wolves in packs demonstrate the importance of teamwork and close family bonds, while the concept of the lone wolf represents the importance of following one's own path and gaining self-knowledge. Rachel Roberts offers practical ways we can use those archetypes both psychologically and magically, using such things as journalling, visualisation, affirmations, and invocations.
Lucya Starza, author of Pagan Portals titles *Candle Magic, Poppets and Magical Dolls, Scrying*, and *Rounding the Wheel of the Year* as well as the novel *Erosion*

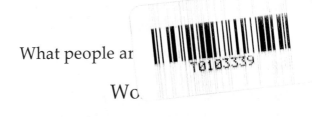

Rachel gloriously weaves the mythological, archetypal, spiritual, and cultural wisdom of the Wolf to empower the reclamation of the lost treasures of our essential nature as women and men! With lore and wisdom, this book will initiate you in living a life of freedom, strength, courage, resilience and wild passion!
Achintya Devi, Founder of Goddess Rising Mystery School

Wolf

Rachel S Roberts

Wolf

Untamed. Courageous. Empowered.
An Inspirational Guide to Embodying
Your Inner Wolf

Rachel S Roberts

MOON
BOOKS
London, UK
Washington, DC, USA

CollectiveInk

First published by Moon Books, 2024
Moon Books is an imprint of Collective Ink Ltd.,
Unit 11, Shepperton House, 89 Shepperton Road, London, N1 3DF
office@collectiveinkbooks.com
www.collectiveinkbooks.com
www.moon-books.net

For distributor details and how to order please visit the 'Ordering' section on our website.

ISBN: 978 1 80341 533 8
978 1 80341 570 3 (ebook)
Library of Congress Control Number: 2023937091

A CIP catalogue record for this book is available from the British Library.

Design: Lapiz Digital Services

UK: Printed and bound by CPI Group (UK) Ltd, Croydon, CR0 4YY
Printed in North America by CPI GPS partners

Contents

This book is dedicated and offered with much love and gratitude to the wolves and wolf essence. It is an honour to be one of your spokeswomen.

And to Grand Mother Wolf and Lupa, who have been my guides and guardians since the beginning. Thank you for being my spiritual mid-wives and showing me the way.

My thanks and gratitude also go to my students and coaching clients that allowed me to share their healing stories in this book. I honour and celebrate you!

Preface

A few years ago, I was sharing about my love of wolves with a long-term student of mine and she exclaimed 'but you are a lion!'.

It is a funny thing when you become associated with a symbol or archetype. However, both wolves and lions have truly always played an important part in my life as my primary guides.

For me the lion has been a masculine presence in my life, especially as my great guardian and protector whom I always imagine chilling out, just lazily basking in the sun, waiting for someone to bring him food, but he will guard me fearlessly and powerfully as soon as called! Lion is also representative of my inner masculine. The inner masculine sometimes is also identified or called the sun aspect of self or your external energy. It is often the confident and sovereign aspect of Lion that is seen by my students when I embody him in teaching and leading, hence the comment made by my student and many others.

No matter our biological gender, within us all is the masculine aspect, and, also the feminine. We relate to these archetypes or aspects within ourselves in different ways, with each aspect having its own woundings, lessons and wisdom. I also believe that we have specific spirit guides to support and guide us with each of these two aspects of self. Perhaps you feel each part of yourself is also personified or represented by a specific animal, plant, guide or guardian. If not yet, I always encourage my students to discover and work with them because they can be your greatest allies when working with inner balance, harmony, integration and the divine marriage within.

In my being, Wolf has always been that which has been prowling, roaming in the darkest and deepest parts of me. She is my fertile earth and cave deep, raw feminine. I could therefore call she-wolf my inner or moon energy, counterpart to my lion-external self. She is the part of me that craves the unfiltered exploration of the womb-tomb mysteries and is fed by uncensored, erotic dance to heavy metal.

For me she-wolf began to howl in my teenage years, around the time I became a belly dance teacher and started reclaiming the sovereignty of my womanhood. At this point in my life, I had a growing awareness of my own sexuality and sensuality as woman. Having witnessed other women and myself being abused, discriminated against or disrespected because we were women, I became passionate about healing the wounds that the feminine had suffered. Finding belly dance at this time was my answer to confusion and self-doubt, and teaching both belly dance and meditation to other women from age sixteen was my destiny. I wanted to inspire other women to also enjoy, love and claim their bodies as theirs, and theirs alone, with self-authority, self-responsibility and self-respect. As I navigated from girl to woman the wolf arose within me with great potency, especially throughout the processes of healing deep woundings in my throat and solar plexus chakras. She-Wolf has since come forth more and more strongly with every step I have taken to nurture myself as an empowered woman.

In me, wolf was ultimately called forth by the need to speak up for the world's injustices, to also speak up for my own needs and rights and when I have needed the courage to be me, unapologetically and truthfully. I have needed wolf courage, wolf ferocity and wolf tenacity on my journey and this energy only became stronger within myself the more I have embraced and embodied the power and value of my feminine self.

I remember being scared of dogs as a young child. I believe that their potential strength frightened me and they represented the wild and untamed that I had been taught was out to get or destroy every young, innocent girl. Ultimately to my younger self the world was full of harm and danger because I had not yet realised or learnt to acknowledge or embrace my own strength, value and worth. I thought I was weak and insignificant. Yet now that I know and declare different, wolf sits comfortably and powerfully within me. My inner wolf, my feminine, has had to fight to survive, she has had to learn courage through assault, betrayal and abandonment. Yet through embodying the perseverance and devotion of the alpha she-wolf, my story has become a true testament that wolf will support you in reclaiming your inner strength and confidence and in trusting in all that you are and can be. In finding this book you are also being called by the wolf within.

I invite you to reflect on *why* wolf has called you and what part of you is feeling or needing the wolf. Do you need her protection and nurturing of your inner child? Do you feel him asking you to be a warrior for a cause? Are you intrigued by something wild and untamed within you or are you facing darkness that you want to better understand or integrate? Why wolf and why now? This book being in your hands is no coincidence.

So, perhaps before we even begin this journey you may want to journal and reflect upon why you are here, and then from there reflect on all the times that wolf has already shown up for you. Not just as a symbol, image or guide but also just for a moment navigate through all the times you were challenged, triggered, healed, needed to be strong, or when you felt powerful. Make a note of anything that comes to mind now. Don't think too much, just make note if an image, experience, word, feeling or resonance arises.

I invite you to come back to these notes at the end of the book and with hindsight you can witness the journey and follow the thread that stemmed from this original enquiry about why you were brought here. Throughout this journey continue to gather together in a journal or mural of some sort, all the seemingly coincidental and miraculous moments, as well as revelations and insights and witness how you were, can be and are truly wolf.

In this book we will explore many different aspects of wolf essence, spirit, archetype and deity and you may find that a certain wolf role or energy appeals or that a theme resonates most powerfully for a situation you are in or a healing that you desire. There is a reason for you reading this book, a personal and unique reason, so continue to be curious as to why your guides or highest self has brought you here. Remember to let go of pre-conceived judgements, as wolf transcends all of the differences and limitations of gender, age and culture that we humans create. In fact, wolves, just like us, all come in different shapes, ages, sizes and colours and will remind you how *all* play a vital and necessary part in the pack.

Whether wolf is a long-term ally that you long to deepen with in different ways, or is completely new to you, whether it resonates with your inner masculine or feminine, or brings together a communion of both, I hope this book supports you in becoming more wolf; that is, loving, wise and courageous.

May this book ultimately be a tool for you to come to know yourself more and empower your true authentic self. I hope that in the most profound and supportive ways it may offer an unveiling or unravelling to bring clarity as to what life, love, fulfilment and purpose uniquely means for you.

With a loving howl from my heart to yours, Rachel

Introduction

Who's afraid of the big, bad wolf? – From The Three Little Pigs.

Wolfish
Adjective
Resembling or likened to a wolf, especially in being rapacious, voracious, or lascivious.

Wolfish
Redefined
Resembling or likened to a wolf, especially in being courageous, intuitive, or untamed.

Throughout our human history wolves have been something to both fear and admire. The wolf is a wild animal, a skilled hunter, ferocious in the defence of its pack and displays intelligence and cunning as well as possessing high organisation skills and a nurturing, affectionate nature.

Yet no other large predator in Europe has been so misunderstood or persecuted. Often when the word wolf is used the image that first comes to mind is the big bad wolf of nursey rhymes or the monster of folktales. I think most people will have encountered in their childhood the deadly wolf of Red Riding Hood or the greedy wolf in the Three Little Pigs. In a lot of European folklore, the Wolf is also a predator to be feared, the bad guy that serves as a warning, or the fate for those that rebel or don't do as they are told. Wolf is also sometimes the nemesis of those who go outside of the safety of the community or the personification of sin or evil. To some extent these ideas were championed because of the need to warn of approaching wild animals that may harm if provoked or threatened. However, the idea that wolves are always highly dangerous, relentlessly vicious or deadly and out to get you, is both scientifically and energetically untrue.

Yet the fear and hatred of wolves is so ingrained in the European psyche and elsewhere in the world, that most humans still have some residue of association of wolf with 'killer', 'death' or 'dangerous' in their unconscious mind, even when they have come to know and love wolves. In some way this is, of course, an instinctual reaction to a predator, much as with lions or tigers. Yet with wolves this unprovoked fear and hatred which we are conditioned in has sadly led to near extinction of their species. It will stop many from giving wolves a chance, to both live and thrive, and to be accepted as a co-existing species that offer us both physical and spiritual support and companionship.

For those of you, like me, who just know the wolf to really be the good guy or just wanted them to be the hero in the story for once, then this book is for you and is a celebration of the wolf as support, guide, protector, hero and muse. It aims to open up to you the true potentiality of wolves and their wisdom, so we can see beyond was had been previously decided or concluded about this multifaceted being.

I am sure I am not alone in being the young girl growing up that admired the wolf of legend and knew there was something deeper or hidden behind the limited perspective we were offered. Perhaps also like me you wanted to run away with the wolves of myth and even had much sympathy for them! The more you come to learn about wolves, the more that you will understand that in reality the wolf you meet in the wild will be wary of you. You may hear them but not see them because they hide from humans. It is us who are actually the most frightening and deadly destroyers on this planet. It is often therefore actually our own fears and destructive nature that we meet in the darkness of the forest, rather than the wolf.

When we come to work with wolves energetically and with the intention of collaboration and communion, we also find that it is the misunderstood 'dangerous' or mysterious qualities of wolf that can be wolf's greatest contribution. It is in many ways their embodiment of that which leads us to deem then unsavoury that makes them invaluable allies for both healing and shadow work. As we will explore in this book, the wolf, undoubtably, does have an association with the darkness, the night time, the unknown, the underworld and the otherworld. Yet it is important to remember, that these associations in themselves do not make the wolf intrinsically wrong or bad.

The dark is part of the paradox of life, one vital half of a reality where dark and light simultaneously exist and ultimately are of the same source. The dark is part of a reality that is so simply complex and imperceptibly obvious that nothing is as it seems and yet everything is as it seems. In order to try and make sense of or understand this reality, however, we condition ourselves to believe that something is always solely one way or another, either good or bad, light or dark, easy or hard. We simplify in an attempt to grasp at something that may always remain outside of our understanding. As students of this reality, however, we will be reminded again and again that all that we make opposing or different is actually one and of the same and that all aspects of life and existence, whether we label them bad or good have value, meaning and contribution. Even the difficult, dark or frightening parts are important, necessary and are irreplaceably powerful!

In hindsight, how often have the darkest times of your life actually been the most insightful or pivotal? Have you ever said 'I just want it to be easy', hoping to skip through the painful parts, to the light and love we believe must be the alternative or other side, only to find that the dark is actually the necessary place where the growth, and insight happens? Have you ever been frightened or even terrified of something that actually when you chose it or did it anyway it became your most pleasurable or perfect way of being or doing? Perhaps you have decided someone was a certain way and then they surprised you by being or acting different to how you expected? How often have you been shown that black and white is more often one hundred shades of grey?

Our ancestors, who lived closer to, as and in nature, I believe knew paradox the way we are only just remembering or accepting. In nature we witness it every second from the necessity of day and night, to the budding of flowers and the falling of leaves. However, in the modern world we are told paradox does not exist, it is always one way or the other. Either you are in, or you are out, either you are good, or bad, you comply or you are punished, you conform or you fail, you are physical or spiritual, but never both or neither. From fear and discrimination of that which is opposite to what we deem right, light or good, we then destroy or reject all that makes us feel unsafe, challenges our perspective or that which is different. We do this from making wrong those of another gender, religion or race, to labelling wolves has dangerous, to even distrusting and shaming our very own uniqueness. In doing so we reject wholeness, completeness and cap allowance in order to validate and retain limitations, conditions and judgement.

Wolf is an exemplary affirmation of the paradox of life; predator yet shy, fierce yet playful, strong yet tender, potential killer yet nurturing, loving pack member. This can pose a challenge to us humans that want a simple answer to, is it good or bad? We know on a physical level that a wild wolf in the forest could kill us just because they are bigger and stronger, yet also instinctively we are drawn to them because on a soul level we know their example and spirit can bring healing, wisdom and divine messages. They could harm us due to their mere physicality but also offer us insight and revelation if we look beyond just their strong legs and sharp teeth. They can additionally offer us powerful lessons about our own paradox's. They show us that by rejecting or condemning wolf, the darkness, the unknown or frightening, we deny the reality of the multifaceted and diverse nature of life, and of the contribution and necessity of life *and* death, shadow *and* light. Whenever we feel we must destroy something merely because it frightens us or is different, Wolf offers us an invitation to see that something as a mirror that is reflecting that we fear or reject within our own self. Wolf asks us not to take action that results in separating ourselves from the whole truth. Wolf can destroy *and* create and so can you. This reminder of our paradoxical nature is reminder of our potentiality and it is also a call to take self-responsibility and to seek self-awareness.

Wolf will remind us through working with them that all aspects of life and experience has power, value and meaning. This is perhaps why Wolf will often arise in our lives and offer collaboration when the shadow or the dark comes up within us, to remind us of the value and gifts *there*. They also show their presence when we are going through times of change and transition so that we can open our eyes and ears to the full spectrum of possibility. As you will discover in this book, Wolves are the great guardians of growth, protection and threshold. Their ability to be and see, above and below, within and without, what was, is and what can be, is an invaluable gift.

They will teach you that fear and love, light and dark, can exist in you harmoniously. You have been taught to run away from paradox but what if you ran with the wolves towards it? What could you learn from your own fears and wounds? Who would you be if you fully accepted and loved all parts of yourself?

Life is a constant engagement with your personal shadow and empowerment comes from a willingness to stand up to the challenge of accepting and integrating it. True living requires you to be willing to be vulnerable, honest and be able to look in the mirror, see the wolf there; all its ferocity, power, and mighty teeth and to not shrink back but to get curious.

What would happen if we always chose to see the whole picture, rather than what we wanted to see, or were told to see? What if we opened our wolf eyes and looked in the darkness of the forest, rather than closing our eyes tight?

As you go through any challenges in life, the dark and the shadow *will* come up because they need to be worked with and they want to be understood so you can consolidate self. They are a part of you, one half that makes you whole and holy, and, are seeking your acceptance and compassion. There are lessons for you in the feared depths of your own inner realms that are ready to be explored and wolves are a powerful ally to stretch your perception of realities to include all possibility. With wolf by your side, you need not fear, fear itself. With wolf by your side, you will strengthen your in-sight and heighten your perception of your own potentiality. They will support you in finding courage.

Wolf's confident guardianship of the dark and unseen realms helps you to navigate those times, places or parts of self that seem tough, uncertain or frightening. They act as a reminder that you can be both gentle and strong, loving and fierce, powerful and compassionate.

Due to these mighty offerings of healing and wisdom, Wolf can be a very fierce energy to work with and so we must approach it with both respect, honour and devotion. Wolf asks that you show up and stand up with courage and determination, and in exchange for their powerful healing and guidance, gratitude and dedication to your purposeful path must be offered. Just as it utilises the diversity of roles and members in the pack, Wolf sees your unique value and contribution and it requires you to recognise it and truly employ it also. Wolf sees and accepts all aspects of you and will not let you waste yourself or your gifts. There is no hiding from any part of yourself or your essentiality when you begin to follow the wolf path.

You will learn to live your life as an essential part of the pack of humanity, no longer lost, searching or frightened but willing and able to contribute your unique essence for the highest good of all.

You are powerful, you are courageous and you are wolf. Welcome home. Welcome to wholeness.

A bit about the scope of this book

This book is an introduction to working with the energy, essence, guides and archetype of the wolf. It is a spiritual guide to enjoying, embracing and embodying the gifts that the wisdom of wolves has to offer. First, we will discover the lessons that earthly wolves share with us, from the idea of the pack and teamwork, to the way their communication skills can inspire us. In part one I will also share with you some real-life examples of how working with Wolf has supported my clients and students, so you can see wolf wisdom applied to every day human situations. We will then move on to briefly explore wolf as totem, symbol and icon in European history and folklore, before diving a little deeper into the messages and codes that lie within wolf story and legend. I hope then to provide some insight into the potent healing and empowerment that wolf connection can bring into your life, through exploring the spirit of wolf and its manifestations of deity, mythological being and spirit guide. I will finish by offering you some ideas for points of connection with Wolf in your everyday life, as well as tips and guidance for ritual, ceremony and holistic practices that will enrich your spiritual practice. This book is a mix of physical, emotional and spiritual guidance that aims to be grounded in ancient belief and nature's wisdom and yet I hope will inspire you to discern and actualise a pathway with wolves that is as unique as you are. I am not here to tell you what to do, but to encourage you to be more of you.

My research of wolf archaeology, deity and history has been mostly European bound, as is also my personal experience, knowledge and background, so the chapters on wolf deities and wolf mythology reflect that. I am aware that the wolf holds great significance in other parts of the world. For example, in both Southern and Northern Native American spirituality and history wolf is a well-known totem and ancestor, just as Shinto also greatly reveres wolves in Japan. However, these specific focuses are not my area of experience or expertise, not because of disinterest but just lack of time and brain capacity! I believe that exploring a worldwide perspective on the significance of wolves in spirituality or history it outside the scope of one book, I would not have the space that I believe is necessary to do it justice! We also do not want to get lost in information overload at the expense of practical embodiment tools and spiritual connection or growth. For these same reasons, this book does not explore the biological history of wolves, nor is it a scientific examination. For as many traditions, stories and cultures that celebrate wolf, there are also as many biological species, subspecies and varieties of wolf and canine family members. For a biological or scientific study of wolves I would highly recommend the research and books of L. David Mech, the world's leading wolf scientist and specialist.[1] However, I will note that, in general, the wolves I discuss in this book are of the grey wolf family, as that is and was the primary wolf species in Europe.

As wolves gradually repopulate this earth and numbers increase from the brink of extinction then wolf knowledge and understanding are ever increasing. Throughout the 20th century as conservation projects, monitoring and studies were put in place, our understanding of wolves increased more than ever. However, much of this understanding was gained from observation of a growing species, sometimes one in captivity or with frequent human interaction. Wolf now is a species that is having to re-learn how to be and live in a world where there is nowhere truly wild anymore. Humans have encroached on all land, either through direct occupation of land, the use or destruction of eco-systems and resources or through our pollution and waste or the desire for instant and always available Wi-Fi. We will now only ever get a glimpse of the potentiality of earth-bound wolves or the wolf that our ancestors knew. We have taken away their freedom and with our increasing human population they will never have it returned. So, in many ways, to know wolf truly as it was and is at its essence, we need to also create a spiritual connection, that which is complemented by but goes beyond solely physical or biological understanding and relations. Unlimited possibility is available to us and Wolf in the energetic memory and the realms beyond human limitations of the mind and logic. Connection to the essence, energy and ancestral imprint of wolves comes forward to fill the gaps so we can gain a complete understanding and knowing of Wolf, as well as gain insight beyond this centuries study wolves and even beyond our own earthbound experiences. I believe that we also must explore and experience alternative ways to connect to wolf. We must find a point of connection that does not negatively impact the living wolf by overly intruding our human selves but can still inspire a deep love and reverence that will take us forward in a holy communion and co-existence with these sacred and beautiful creatures. What would be possible if we truly knew and felt wolf in our hearts *and* souls? What can we learn from their wisdom and lives when we choose to let go of the obstacles and conditions that we humans create? It is this spiritual connection that this book seeks to facilitate.

The spiritual essence and energy of Wolf is beyond any barriers or borders. Being of divine source is it not bound by our human limitations of time, space, gender, language or cultural background. Therefore, the words shared here are spoken in celebration, gratitude and honour of all wolves and the chapters other than those mentioned above include tools, messages and symbology from all wolves in general, both physical and spiritual and from Wolf essence.

No matter where in the world we are from, Wolf is within us, on a cellular and energetic level. There is a vast intelligence and potential available to you no matter your age, background, life situation or experiences. Wolf was here in this realm and on this earth prior to human existence and have been our guides and guardians ever since we arrived. Their spirit is here from alpha to omega, to teach us what it means to be, to love, to live, to remember, to create. The way of the wolf is ultimately a path of deepening into your inner wisdom and intuition. It is an awakening and remembrance of yourself as, of and from the earth, stars and the divine.

To support you in this, throughout this book there will be suggestions for practical activities as well as prompts for ritual and journalling. So, I would advise you to have a dedicated journal, notebook or art pad especially for this journey with Wolf. Your presence here and your reading of this book is an offering towards Wolf, a way of witnessing, honouring and saying thank you for all that it is. It is also a promise and a devotional act of taking sacred time for communion and I believe even just this in itself will make a huge difference to and for Wolf.

So, thank you, and let us begin!

NB. Throughout this book I choose to refer to the Divine aspect of Wolf as ***Wolf Essence***, which could also be called Wolf Spirit, Wolf Soul or Divine wolf. I also use ***Wolf*** as an all-encompassing umbrella term for all aspects and manifestations of Wolf and wolves, from earth-bound wolves to spirit wolves to the idea of Wolf.

Opening sacred space with Wolf

This book is an awakening of and connection to your inner wolf, wolf wisdom and essence. This journey is a holy one, a ritual of communion that requires your courage, presence and devotion to growth. I therefore invite you now to open sacred space for all that you are about to learn, remember and activate. Use this moment to set an intention or promise to show up for yourself and your healing, in all the ways you desire and deserve.

Take time to light a candle, sit or lie comfortably and breathe deeply. Then speak aloud or read this opening invocation, prayer or manifesto as your pledge to yourself that you are ready to embrace all the ways in which you can learn from Wolf.

I . . . (and say your name)
Call on wolf essence, my wolf guides and guardians . . . (you can add any other specific guides)
As witness, as protection, as guide,
As I open sacred and holy space for this powerful embodiment journey with wolf.
I pledge to honour my path and be present to every step, moment and experience.
I promise to show up for myself,
To hold myself with love and compassion,
And with allowance for all that I am and can be,
Without judgement or criticism.
I am willing now to step into this empowering journey and deepen my knowledge of self.
I remember that I am the point of creation and destruction.
So, I take full self-responsibility for myself,
And I acknowledge that the power to create, manifest, heal or change that which I wish,

Lies in my hands, my heart and my choice.
With wolf as my guide, guardian and protector,
I run forward with my pack.
I move towards the fulfilment of my destiny, purpose and passion.
Howling my truth, embodying trust,
I declare that I am present here now, as me, for me, and I am enough.
I am wolf.
And so, it is and so it will be. Blessed be.

Part I

Discovering Wolf

Chapter 1

Wolf spirit as embodied by the living Wolf

Father Wolf taught him his business, and the meaning of things in the jungle, till every rustle in the grass, every breath of the warm night air, every note of the owls above his head, every scratch of the bat's claws as it roosted for a while in a tree and every splash of every little fish jumping in the pool meant just as much to him as the work of his office means to a businessman.
– The Jungle Book, Rudyard Kipling

We begin with introducing and exploring the contribution and wisdom offered by earth bound wolves; those that live and roam as physical beings on this planet.

The wolf species are an inspiration and a guide to us primarily around the themes of family, teamwork, and communication. They show us how to live and work in community, how to utilise and contribute our unique skills and experience and how to be fierce and protect, as well as gently loving and considerate. To us, they can be a symbol of strength, intuition and determination, all of which can connect us with our personal power. We witness their courage and strength and feel it arise within ourselves.

The life of a wolf is one that requires it to step into many roles, such as hunter, parent, teacher and leader. Many of their roles are ones that we also share in common and it can help us in our own lives to follow their example. They teach us how practice makes progress and how adaptability and patience are vital to growing into and flourishing in any role or position in life. The Wolf can be both fierce predator with the potential to kill when needed and also nurturing, playful and loving, with the potential to create and nourish.

Wolves are also known to be highly sociable and they live in close and affectionate packs who enjoy play and singing. They seek and nurture companionship, even sometimes during the lone wolf stage of their life. They often seek physical contact with each other, nuzzling and cuddling and communicate frequently for fun as well as necessity. They are also skilled hunters, with powerful senses and strong bodies as well as highly intelligent minds. Ultimately wolves show themselves to be gentle, affectionate, playful, loyal and protective. Along with the powerful gifts of insight and instinct, devotion and determination I believe Wolves really are super heroes.

Both as individuals and as a pack they offer us certain lessons and wisdom that can be potent when applied to our own lives. So here in this chapter we will start with exploring the lessons that are offered to us by the wolf pack as a whole and then move onto the individual members, roles and considerations within it.

As we do so reflect on and bring awareness to where and how the themes relate and resonant in your own life. What would support you to emulate? What are you most inspired by or wish to recreate? How can you embody their example and channel the strengths and wisdom of wolves?

LESSONS OF THE PACK

For the strength of the pack is the wolf, and the strength of the wolf is the pack. – Rudyard Kipling

The Wolf Pack

When it comes to wolves, some of the most powerful insights can be gained from witnessing their family mechanisms and behaviour patterns within the family unit. Their various roles in the pack remind us that we all have a gift to offer, that every part makes the whole and that when we contribute our authenticity and uniqueness, we are in fact offering our greatest support to our pack, on both a small and global scale.

Wolves live in small packs of between two and twenty animals, most of whom are related. Wolf packs are not formed just to hunt or for hunting strategy but rather are primarily family units that remain together for companionship and education. The size of the pack is based on the availability of food and resources and when more prey is available larger groups can stay together more efficiently than if prey were scarce. They generally keep a strict hierarchy with roles that allow the wolves to work as a team and a unit during both domestic times and hunting. The whole pack is also involved in the raising and teaching of pups. The old, sick and wounded are included and cared for in the pack, and brought food by other pack members, they are never abandoned. Looking after all pack members no matter, their age or physical capability is one of the characteristics of wolves that can most profoundly touch and inspire us. All pack members interact with each other frequently, confirming bond and affection.

When it comes to leadership of a wolf pack it is most often not about competition or domination! The Alpha pair of the pack are the mother and the father wolf. The she-wolf will mate with a wolf, producing a bunch of offspring once a year who become the rest of the pack. When in their second or third year some pups will leave to create their own pack. They become a lone wolf until they find a mate and then their pups become their pack. In this way the breeding pair become the natural leaders, just like humans pairing up to create a family and then creating a nucleus around them of children and grandchildren.

Unlike large cat males who will kill the cubs of predecessors, or even sometimes their own offspring, male wolves are noted for their particularly paternal instincts. In general alpha and father wolves show affection for pups and other pack members, and have even been known to adopt the pups of other wolves or from other packs. They take a vested interest in the survival of every pack member and will tend to pups diligently, offering us an example of the masculine in its mightiest role of protector and facilitator of growth and life. Male wolves shown us that is possible to be strong and gentle, powerful and caring.

Lessons of the Pack

We can and will move through various roles and stages in our own lives. There are times when we need to be leader, times when we need to be mother and times when we are student or newbie. None is better or more important than the other. Wolf teaches us the value of each in its own time and place. All of us always have something to teach and something to learn.

At the same time, it is you that must determine how you make your contribution to the pack. It is important to align with your innate truth and divine purpose and offer that. No-one else can tell you who you are or what you should do, nor are you just a replica or result of your parents, your friends, or your society. You are not the expectations placed upon you. You have your own essential nature and must find your own unique way of being. You, as distinctive and different as you are, is what is vital and most needed. It has been a wound of the patriarchy that has led us to believe that we can only achieve by getting to the top, that ultimate power is to dominate all literal and metaphorical hierarchies. However, our true power and contribution comes when we honour ourselves and give from a place humility, allowance, truth and trust.

The pack teaches us that we must take self-responsibility for our actions, thoughts and words and honour our weaknesses as well as our strengths. We are the point of creation and the point of destruction and true strength comes from knowing and accepting all parts of ourself with compassion rather than judgement. We and our unique frequency are the greatest contribution we can make.

The entire pack also contributes to and has responsibility for rearing wolf pups and so we are all responsible for the growth, well-being and safety of our human-family. The young and vulnerable are always to be protected and supported as our first priority and the focus of most of our resources, time and energy.

Our family or pack, is also not just our biological relations, but can be our friendship circles and wider community instead or as well as. We need a pack around us for support, affection and well-being, but a pack must be where we can give and receive respect, honesty and unconditional love. Seek it, find it and then treasure it. There is immeasurable value to be found in being with and listening to others, as well as slowing down for nourishing time that has no agenda but mutual joy. Your pack will support your growth, never hinder it and relationships take commitment, devotion and mutual loving intention to prosper.

Alpha – Wolf as Leader

The biggest, strongest and most ferocious, is not how a leading wolf is 'chosen'. The leaders of a pack are always a mating pair, with the leading female topping the pack hierarchy. It is the she-wolf that is the highest authority in the pack, even the alpha male will take his lead from her, though often they will make decisions together. The leading pair are almost always the only breeding pair in a pack and in creating the pack by becoming a couple, they are the first breeding pair of that pack and the pack will mostly consist therefore of their offspring. The function of the leading pair ultimately is to guide and protect the younger wolves. They use discernment and the wisdom from their experience to make decisions. However, when appropriate or needed other wolves within the pack may take on the role of leader in a certain situation. In general, there are no fights for leadership in wild wolf packs. What is needed for a pack leader to be effective is experience in the current context or activity and although the leading parent pair will have ultimate responsibility and leadership of the pack, in their wisdom, there are times when they know to allow others wolves to offer their unique skills and abilities.

For example, when navigating through snow, the biggest and strongest wolves will lead at the front, acting as a plough and creating a trail for the other wolves to follow. They do so, not to show off their superiority but in the creation of a safe and clear way they offer their unique skills to help the others. They are pathway makers for the younger and smaller wolves that are behind. The biggest and strongest wolves are not always the parents. The alphas may sometimes even stay behind while the biggest wolves plough ahead and return to the front of the line if needed, such as in times of suspected danger or when the way does not need to be cleared.

If the leaders are not determined by being aggressive or dominating, they are by being ultimately responsible, just as any mum and dad are for their family unit of children. Another of their primary functions is to maintain and encourage harmony.

The leading pair will continue to breed every year and new pups are born in the spring. Litters are between four and six pups and they will receive care from both parents as well as guidance from older siblings. Wolves most often practice monogamy with their mate for life, or until one of them dies and seem to greatly grieve the loss of their partners.

When a leading wolf becomes too old to lead the pack, or becomes badly injured, the next dominant wolf will take over. The old or weak are not ousted but are still loved and cared for in the pack. They will in effect retire but are still respected and appealed to for the wisdom and experience they have to offer.

Lesson of Alpha

Leadership is not about ruling over, but ruling for and wisdom comes from experience, experience being the alchemical process that turns knowledge into wisdom.

The leadings wolves teach you to acknowledge what you don't know just as much as you do know. Leadership is not about dominance but that your skills, knowledge or experience suit leadership in that particular context and time. How to be a leader is as diverse as potential situations. The leader as an infant school teacher is just a valuable as, but requiring a different approach to, a leader as a motivational speaker or project manager. All leadership roles contain the same essence of inspiring and facilitating creation and growth.

Wolves share with us the knowing of when we are required to be in the role of leader and when being a leader would be the best use of our skills and knowledge. They can also teach us to recognise the knowing of when it is time to not be Alpha. There are times when you will be called to embody leadership and organisational qualities and other times when humility or instinct will remind you that you would best serve the pack in a supportive or learning role.

As leader we need to have both an understanding of and the ability to use both our inner masculine and inner feminine, recognising the value of each and exploring how they work together more effectively than they do alone. Harmonic union, collaboration and integration internally also allows for the same successful facilitation externally.

What are the ultimate defining features of a strong alpha or pack leader? Clear communication, self-awareness, community before individuality, and the allowance and celebration of the uniqueness of each pack member.

Mother Wolf

Wolf Mothers are generally ferociously protective, clever leaders and loving teachers. The Mother wolf is one half of the pack leadership, along with her male mate but she can also lead a pack on her own. Ultimately all of the most important decisions for the pack are made by the lead female.

She is thorough in providing for her young and more mature children, as well as in preparation for the birth of cubs. Many months before she is due to give birth a mother wolf will instinctively search out a suitable den, making sure it offers both protection and is near water. She will use great discernment and hollow out a specific area called a nest which she will protect from intruders, flooding and the cold. She may return to the same den many times over her lifetime. When she has new born pups she is the priority and centre of the whole pack and she receives their support, food and attention so she can expend her energy into what it is she is growing. After weaning and as the pups grow, mother wolves return to hunting and the care of pups continues to be facilitated by the whole pack.

Lesson of Mother

The most valuable lesson of Mother Wolf is to allow yourself to receive. It is often expected that a mothering role is one that primarily gives, in fact it is the opposite. Being able to mother requires you to be able to receive, as in order to give you must have something to give. If mother wolf did not receive the food, company and protection of her pack she would not be able to birth or raise her children successfully or healthily.

How are you at receiving? How often have you placed conditions, limitations and judgements on what you should or could receive and so cut yourself of from being supported, nourished or provided for, whether spirituality, emotionally or physically? What if you were to truly open to receiving and to all that is possible when you allow yourself to be loved and nurtured unconditionally?

At the same time, Mother wolf reminds you that you do have a choice about what and how you receive and you will know, when you trust instinct, what is truly right and supportive for you. No one else can tell you what you are feeling or needing, you must own your self-authority and you must communicate your needs. What are your expectations of others and can you take full responsibility for what, when and how you ask for help, support, guidance or attention?

Mother is biological but can also be a non-gendered role, with no need to birth a child to be able to embody the role of mother. Male wolves are just as loving, caring and protective of pups as the females. You can also provide a mothering role to a team, to land, to a plant, a cat or birth/create a project, a book, a business, a home. All are valid and needed.

Sometimes being Mother is also not about feeding or cleaning, sometimes it is about offering those younger an example to follow of someone who knows and practices self-care, self-compassion, and self-fulfilment. A mother feeds her children with her example, just as much as with her milk. Mother wolf makes her den for her own comfort just as much as for her pups. She knows that if she is in her best place physically and emotionally, then she can all the better fulfil her task of birthing and nursing.

Time in the Cave

The mother wolf knows when it is time to retreat. She knows and honours when it is time to make space and create a place for her to *be*. She knows that she must give her full energy into incubation and pregnancy. She knows when it is time to be nourished and to go within. She trusts her instinct and listens to her body. She does not withdraw because she is forced but because she is well practised in knowing what she needs and answers the call. Wolf mothers may create a den within a cave, in a natural hole, under overhanging tree roots, in the ground, or under rocks. She often knows this place well and will return to it year after year, keeping it clean and ready. The den can be used by many generations of female wolves.

Lesson of the cave

Your body is intelligent and intuitive. It is a powerful resource and it constantly giving you messages and signs. How are you at listening? That headache is not annoying or inconvenient, it is your body saying stop, listen, it is a loving request to do, be different, to acknowledge something or create change, or rest.

The she-wolf recognises the need to ground, to be deep in the earth, held by dark, winter, the beneath and the great below. As women we retreat into the cave with our cycle every month and know that we physically and emotionally need this essential time of rest and rejuvenation to keep ourselves healthy and happy for the rest of the cycle. Yet all genders can benefit from recognising and listening to our bodies, minds and souls and acknowledging when they are in need of rest and care. We also all need times of inward reflection and introspection.

It is important to be reminded of the power of being (feminine) in this world that praises and honours doing (masculine).

The feminine is cyclical and she (the feminine part of all of us) needs the "winter phase" of cycles in order to enter the cave of darkness, replenish and sometimes give death to, in order to them create anew and then rebirth.

The void, that is held within the retreat of the den, is the space in which we can focus our energy inwards and listen. We must trust this time, and let it run its course. This is the time for doing nothing, or for reflecting, planting seeds, letting go or for giving space for inspiration to come through.

Spring will come again with the time to birth anew and summer will also come again for action, external growth. Time in the cave will restore you or inspire you before your steps forward. The wolf mothers and grandmother wolves will hold you in this place. Female wolves have made this return to the darkness of the cave since the beginning of time, as have the women of your lineage and ancestry. Trust that there is a knowing within the feminine of all of us that holds the deepest wisdom of receptivity and creation. From the retreat into the cave, you can then act and do from a place that you have cultivated, strengthened and nourished within your own inner depths.

Beta and Omega

Alpha being first in the Greek alphabet refers to the first leading pair that mate and then produce pups. The betas are then the first litter of pups from the leading pair and the omegas any younger pups in subsequent years. One of the biggest misinterpretations of the pack and wolf mentality is that the pack is dominated by a masculine Alpha, who controls his subservient and submissive betas and omegas. In truth, in the wolf pack, no one is insignificant or in any way of a lesser value. If the largest, strongest wolves lead at the front in the snow it is because their skills lie in shovelling a path, enabling other wolves to conserve their energy for contributing their own skills. It would really make no sense at all to send the pups in front to navigate unknown areas and wolves being highly intelligent animals know when and how to utilise their skills for the benefit of all.

The roles of beta and omega teach us not submission but to accept when we are less experienced and to seek that experience with the guidance and support of those more experienced (the alphas). For the wolves experience comes mostly with age, their time as Beta and Omega is time exploring and navigating what it is the be wolf and how they be and do in the world. Their first few hunts may not be quite as effective as they hoped, but they don't give up. They try again and again and keep learning, years if it takes that, before they hone their skills. The older pups and elders which teach the younger pups as it is only when you have been through something and truly know it, breathed it, felt that, that you can teach another to navigate that same journey.

Knowledge and wisdom don't necessarily come with age, and it certainly isn't linked to gender, but rather from experience.

Some wolves may be great at hunting, some may be good at babysitting, others might be great singing teachers and some are the experts of sleeping. Likewise, you may be the Alpha in plumbing skills but an absolute pup when it comes putting up a tent or vice versa. You do not become an expert in anything from one training course, reading one book or baking a cake once!

It takes repeated experience, devotion and dedication to learning and a good dose of curiosity and humility. These are the skills of Beta and Omega and you will see them displayed by the wolf pups as they move out of pup age and into their second and third years.

Lesson of Beta and Omega

A family unit of mutual support and consideration is essential to the harmony of the family and to the healthy and successful growth of all. Pack life and social interaction is vitally important to the health and well-being of wolves and humans. We are not alone, we are never alone, even when we feel lonely. Never forget that you are part of families of friendship, of the packs of earth, the plants, the animals, the cosmos, humanity. You are cared for and supported at all times, even when you can't or don't understand life or the ways in which it weaves.

Family also goes far deeper than blood. Soul family is truly created not by obligation or guilt but choice and honouring and respecting the truth of self and others. You do not owe your loyalty to anyone just because they share your blood. If someone makes you feel small, stupid, or wrong, they are not your family. Family is created by mutual trust, respect, healthy boundaries, consideration and non-judgement.

In life all roles and skills are valuable and needed. Finding our place within the pack, as well as our unique role and contribution can take time and experiment. Your destiny is no one else and the journey it takes is individually distinctive. No one speaks, thinks, walks, creates like you do. You do have a place and you do have an important purpose and there is no time limit for searching for that. There is also no time limit for or just one way of discovering who you are and what you uniquely offer.

I say to my dance students again and again, practice makes progress, and progress is more important than perfection. If you must, aim only for your own perfection, as your perfect is not relative to any other. You will never be your teacher, so don't try to be, your experiences will be different even if you resonate with their approach or results! A great teacher will not mould you in their own image and they will give you guidance, rather than rules.

Beta and Omega Wolf teaches us that harmony comes from retaining a sense of self and individuality, while also belonging to a pack that feels right for us and that is in alignment with our true values and desires.

Lone Wolf

A lone wolf is generally one that is wanting or needing to branch out from its current pack and make its own way. Wolves will avoid incest and so to mate, they need to leave their pack of relations or wait for a passing and handsome stranger. At around two to three years old when the next generation of pups has arrived, or if food is scarce, one or two wolves may go out to start their own families. They are not often lone wolves for a long period of time, just several months. They will spend this time alone looking for another lone mate with which to start a new pack and will explore establishing their own territory, sometimes travelling great distances to find their place to make a home. When two lone wolves find each other, they will bond by beginning a courtship of tail waggling and nose touching. It is, however, known, though rare, for some wolves to remain lone wolves or to travel great distances and spend a long time alone. It is unusual because time alone can be a vulnerable position for any wolf to be in but they will sometimes go to great lengths to find the place they are meant to be in, or the wolf they want to be with. Perseverance and patience are the themes of the Lone Wolf.

Lesson of the Lone Wolf

The lone wolf reminds us of the necessity of time on our own and the creation of our own unique identity. Solitude is often needed to deepen our connection to self. If the thought of being alone seems scary to you, remember that you are never truly alone in anything. You have the divine, your guides, nature and yourself with you at all times, supporting you, loving you, looking out for you.

Time alone and independent thinking can be essential in forming how we are as a person and in listening to our true soul's resonance. Society or family upbringing may feel like the defining mould of who we are but it is vital to branch out, like the lone wolf, and search for and create our own definition of self. It takes courage to do so, but wolves are known for their ferocity and can guide you showing up for yourself with devotion and dedication.

This idea of adventure and seeking may feel like that which belongs to a young person, but again age being a barrier is a judgement we had created, not truth. You may need time as a lone wolf at any age and at any point in your life. It is the time of transition, change, expansion, contraction or may involve a rite of passage. For example, a lone wolf period of life may be for you the time between jobs when you are really refining and realigning where or what it means to be fulfilled. Or you may have lived in the same home for over forty years but feel it is the right time to go and find that dream cottage on the beach the other side of the world, so you begin the search and let your heart lead you on a journey.

Lone wolf teaches you to truly learn how to be and radiate your truth, your authenticity and carve the time to discover what makes you, you. When you shine brightly your inner light, as scary as that may seem, there are those that will see that light and adore it, value it, and celebrate it. Holding the imitation of another's light will always be dimmer and will never be quite the right fit. Be wolf courageous in your quest for self and even more courageous in the sharing of it.

Wolf Cubs

The average pack of three to nine, produces around six pups a year. Wolf cubs are born completely blind and as their ears are folded over their foreheads, they also struggle to hear in their first few weeks. They are completely dependent on their mother and pack for food, warmth and safety. The cubs are the central heart of the pack and protected by all. The den is therefore the social centre of the pack and pack territory. As they grow up the whole pack continues to care for, tend and teach the pups. They learn by imitating their older siblings and parents. Playtime is their practice for honing their hunting skills, with a stick, feather or stone taking the place of prey. The pack is effectively a school and often wolves will stay with their parents well into their second and third years of life to as Wolf researcher Mech says, *'increase the opportunity for offspring to learn the more subtle components of hunting foraging behaviour that are not innate.'*[2] Wolves may have a physical advantage when it comes to hunting but there is still much knowledge to be learnt from their parents, just as we are born essentially human but learn speech, behaviour, values and emotional response from our parents.

Pups may stay in the pack for life. If there is surplus food and prey abundant than this behaviour is common, as for the wolves it is better that any spare food goes to their own offspring rather than it to be wasted or left to others. If the parents or pack can provide much food, then pups may remain within the pack for many years, as they will be well fed and can also grow strong and healthy. When some pups are ready, around two to three years old, they may leave to create their own path, becoming a lone wolf until they form their own pack. If food is scarce, with little to go around, then pups may leave a lot earlier but this does lessen their chance of growing strong and healthy.

Lesson of the Wolf Cubs

Know when you need to ask or receive help and surrender to it. The art of receiving is the art of surrendering. Surrendering or letting go does not make you weak or deem you incapable but rather it is an act of honesty and trust. In many ways, like the pups we are blind in this world and experience will open our eyes, but it is the alchemical transformation of knowledge into wisdom, via experience, that enables us to see. This takes time, patience, reflection, openness and allowance.

There is no shame in that we very often need help. nor should you be embarrassed at needing guidance. Everyone at some point starts as a beginner and sometimes no one knows the answers but the divine! There is also no shame or wrongness in learning being a fun, playful and enjoyable process. In fact, what lights you up, brings you pleasure and joy is absolutely the path of learning that you should follow! When did we decide that learning should always be hard? Approach life and learning with curiosity, not guilt, obligation or self-doubt and know that you are supported every step of the way. Some lessons may be tougher than others and when learning to run you may fall over the same twig a few times, but the divine and the wolves will lend a hand in getting you to your feet again.

From research it has been found the wolves have a vast variance in coming into maturity. They can leave the pack from anywhere between ten months to five years after birth. Let this remind you that we are not ready when we are told we should be, but when we know it or feel within ourselves. Have full allowance for the individuality of yourself and others, in learning and in life. We all have our own skills, gifts and path and we all take our own unique time and way in finding them. Learn the patience of wolves through practising it.

It is also valuable to reflect on the difference and subtle edges between what it is we learn from our parents and society and what is innate to us. It is important to discern between the two so that we can fully align with our own truth while also seeing the wisdom or limiting conditions that has been passed down to us. Not all that is given to you, can benefit or support you, even if given in love. What if you stripped away everything not 'chosen' by you, what would be left? Who are you, truly? Take that essential self to all your roles in life and return to that essential self when you step out of them at the end of the day. Remember that you are a soul, first and foremost, rather than just a role or label. Grow into your pack or partnerships as an individual wolf, discern the edges between you and them and bring your wholeness of self to all that you do and be.

The Way Wolves Hunt

Wolves are omnivores, eating both plants and animals with a diverse diet and adaptability to their circumstances, season and food source availability. They can eat anything from fruit, berries, birds, insects to stags, although, of course, the ideal meal is the larger mammals that can provide for the whole pack in one sitting and fill up the belly for longer.

Hunting animal prey in a risky and expensive business that proves both difficult and dangerous for Wolves, which I think is the most likely reason that we view wolves as both incredibly fearsome and determined! Wolves, however, are also very discerning and will hunt down mostly injured animals, or those that are weak, old or young. Being highly-skilled and sensitive hunters, they will not only take in the physical condition of potential prey but also can sense and consider the psychological state. With the pack in mind, they consider the chance of a successful attack, as failure would mean suffering for all. They will hunt for many, many miles to find a source of food, showing perseverance and great stamina.

Wolves will sometimes hunt as a pack, each with their own role to fulfil. The task they fulfil is based on their natural skills and experience, whether that be as attacker and killer or those that can drive and direct the prey. The breeding pair is often the pair who will hunt, as they are the oldest and so most experienced, then their pups will join them when they are older. A group is not necessarily needed for the hunt, lone wolves can hunt alone successfully and single wolves will hunt on behalf of the pack, for example, father wolf when his partner is nursing their first pups. Studies suggest that one hunter or a pair actually kills more prey than a pack, though the prey will be smaller. A pack is needed for some larger mammals. The old, very young and babysitters will remain back at the den and often food is bought to them. Sometimes a group of wolves will split for hunting if their food is scarcer or widely dispersed, so you will have in this case two hunting packs.

One of the reason wolves may choose to hunt in a pack is to ensure that any kill is kept for the pack, with the consideration that other predators may have to be driven away. This is done in order to ensure that the young will get their share as well and that there is enough food to feed everyone, including pups and elderly. The pack effectively asks as a bodyguard at the buffet. However, once the wolves have had their fill, only taking what they need, they will leave the carcass for other animals and birds to take their share. There is an extremely large ecosystem that forms around prey and many animals rely on the wolf to provide them with food, from bacteria, to bugs to bears and ravens.

Lesson of the Hunt

Wolves are such a powerful example of sticking power. They teach us to see things through, approaching life, our projects, our relationships and growth with determination and passion. However, the wolf sees clearly and make informed decisions. They know when a kill is not worth making, they know when it is better to say 'not this time'. They ask you to cleverly access and weigh up, listening and considering the perspective of your mind, body and soul. They encourage you to ask 'does this really contribute to my soul's path, my heart's joy or the benefit of humanity?'.

They also offer a reminder that sometimes a no is not a never, it is sometimes 'not now', 'for later' or 'the time just isn't right'.

When knowing the scent to follow in life, when knowing where to aim your arrow of direction or focus, trust your instincts and intuition. Also, trust YOUR WHY as the fire that fuels you. What is the reason that you want this, what are fighting for, what drives you, motivates you? If it is truly aligned, if your heart and soul want, or need it and it is a part of your path and purpose, then you will make it happen. If either your body, mind, heart or soul is not on board, you may feel resistance or need to return to base to check in and listen to that part of you. Self-sabotage or procrastination can both be your inner knowing telling you that something isn't aligned or ripe, it could also be an attempt by your highest self to steer you away or it can be a result of self-doubt or mistrust of self. Be curious about which it is.

The hunting wolf also reminds you that you achieve for you and achieve for the all. Wolves are like a sports team, with consideration for others, watching and observing where their team mates are, ultimately so you are successful together. The goal for the wolves or any team is not personal fame, but a collective achievement. It is about finding a balance with that which fulfils you and that which offers too other. An imbalance either way will either lead to you feeling dissatisfied and resentful, or a disconnection between you and community, that will be lesser than for the lack of your contribution. We truly do shine brighter together but also need to maintain our own light to have something to contribute.

Strength

Wolves often will hunt prey that is large, fast and weighty, such as deer, wild goat and sheep, as well as elk, bison and ox. Their physical potential is such that they could kill another animal up to ten times their own weight. They bring prey down with their strong jaws and strong, agile legs. It is not actually their bite that is deadly but they play to their greatest assets, their powerful legs that are used for long distant, often sustained running, as well as digging, swimming and jumping. They use their stamina to tire out their prey.

Their strength is essential for survival but wolves are not senseless killers, their strength is used with consideration. They will stand their ground with ferocity but are also known to by shy, cautious animals that are not known to attack humans nor to attack unprovoked. Their greatest strength actually lies not in their physicality but their communication skills, which are honed and used with clarity and consideration. Wolves rarely fight amongst themselves because their communication which each other is so effective.

Lessons of strength

Strength is not the same as force. To force is to push something beyond what it is meant to do or be. Force lacks the wisdom of strength that knows when it is best used, contained or shared. Wolf has a deep awareness of its own abilities and the necessity of when and where to use its strength. Strength is a gift given to be able to support and serve the pack, whether wolf or human.

Strength is also not created by defeating or dominating others. Strength is sourced from deep within, beyond the physical and not relational to other. Strength is a cord that runs through the centre of our body connecting us to the depths of the earth and the far reaches of the cosmos. Strength comes from grounding, it is deep within and holds us on course, keeps us running towards our northern star when times seems tough. It is also the ability to let ourselves be held, to hold others when they need it and the wisdom and endurance to again and again embrace change, redirection and pivots.

Many times, students have come to me ashamed that their kindness is a weakness. In a society that is increasingly selfish and inconsiderate, kindness is POWERFUL, it is courageous, and the ripples it creates are immeasurably potent and long lasting. Kindness is a true and mighty strength. Kindness is also not self-sacrificing or selfish but rather it is giving without fear of judgement or rejection. It is sharing yourself, your gifts or your compassion and love without the sole expectation or requirement to receive something in return. Imagine the healing for humanity and this planet is people were more kind to each other and themselves.

I think one of the most beautiful moments in Kipling's Jungle Book is when Father Wolf presents the human child Mowgli to Mother Wolf in the Wolf Den. Kipling writes 'A wolf accustomed to moving his cubs can, if necessary, mouth an egg without breaking it, and though Father Wolf's jaws closed right on the child's back not a tooth even scratched the skin, as he laid it down among the cubs.'[3] *For me this moment displays so wonderfully the paradoxically potentiality of wolf; both gentle and fierce, strong, yet delicate.*

Boundaries

There are clearly defined boundaries within wolf territories so that all can eat and have access to prey. The howling of a pack can indicate to other packs, the location of a pack or wolf and sometimes also act as warning. Scent marking works in much the same way, with the boundary it creates offering a way to avoid conflict and offers a reminder of who and what is where. Wolves will leave twice as many scent marks around the edge of the territory as they do at its core. Each scent mark is approximately two hundred and forty metres apart and will last around three weeks. Boundaries are established from the beginning, so as to save energy later on, basically as a preventative of fights. They also offer security to the pack. Having boundaries also enforces their sense and understanding of home and belonging. Boundaries are a form of protection, as well as defence. When a new pair find a location for a den they will straight away assess and create boundaries. Pack boundaries can change and adapt as the pack does, moving with them and as they split, grow or decline in number or generation.

Lessons of boundaries

Wolf in this way offers us a lesson on establishing and upholding clear and healthy boundaries. Their wisdom is for us to know when boundaries serve and support, coming from alignment with truth, and, those that came from woundings, trauma or fear and cause suffering or detriment to ourself or others.

It would not serve the pack to keep everyone and everything out, yet it also does not serve to let everyone and everything in.

It is important that we are responsible for creating our boundaries and do not allow others to make or influence them. Check in with yourself frequently and reinforce, modify or change them. Are they still needed? Are they helpful? Are they respectful or both yourself and others? Boundaries change just as we and our needs do.

Boundaries when used healthily can affirm our self-assurance and self-trust.

Use them wisely. The boundaries or barriers we create when wounded or in trauma, are often the same ones that will later on keep out love, support and surrender. Boundaries flow both ways and often that which we put in place to protect from invasion can sometimes prevent us from also expanding. Wolves will check to see if scent marks marking boundaries are old or fresh and explore, or avoid territory as appropriate. What boundaries are outdated for you? What boundaries need reaffirming?

Wolves also can teach you have to learn, through practice and utilising inner wisdom and intuition, how to communicate your boundaries effectively. How does it feel good for you to share your boundaries? Do you need speak to yourself in a more loving, gentle way, or do you need to add some healthy structure or will power to your daily habits? Or do you need to remove yourself from a situation or person for a while? Do you need to expand into a different or new experience? Do you need to talk to someone calmly and one to one, or do you need to be firmer and clearer? How do you address a strong boundary with a group as compared to be an intimate boundary with a lover?

Remember that boundaries can be made physically, energetically, spiritually and emotionally.

Client example of Wolf Pack teachings and healings.

A client of mine came to me for support because she wanted to increase her self-confidence. She was not happy about the size or shape of her body. During a dance activation workshop with me she realised that her body did not feel like hers, it felt almost like it belonged to someone else. It was not that she considered herself overweight but that she just didn't feel fully herself.

During our sessions my client shared that she was mostly healthy in what she ate but she created the daily meals she ate from the recipe book and habits that she had been given to her by her mother. On diving deeper into her relationship with food and weight, we discovered that her weekly visit to her mum's house for Sunday lunch also brought up its own problems. You see, her mum, through her desire to nourish was a food pusher. Food was her mum's realm, where she could share her skills and love, provide for her family and receive celebration and gratitude from her family. So, every Sunday my client would eat piles of food, every last bit, even if she didn't like it. Her mum would encourage her to eat more, comment that she would soon get too skinny if she didn't eat up and the big one, we all hear, that there are starving people in the world and we are bad if we don't eat the food we are so lucky to have. More than a few plates later my client would not only feel heavy with food, but heavy with guilt and resentment.

At home this continued, the recipe book from her mother created portions that were big and though living alone she had to create and finish every last bit of any meal so nothing was wasted and her mother would approve. Though in her forties, she was still the wolf pup being fed by her childhood pack.

She realised through our work together that she was the shape that would make her mother happy. She was validating her mother by eating lots of food, but in doing so was betraying herself. We discovered that she was keeping herself metaphorically smaller than her mother; as to make her own choices about what she ate, would mean expanding beyond what her mother had chosen and created, which felt like rejecting her mother. Although having moved away from her physical home in her late teens she was still in many ways living within the confines of her mother's pack. She needed to embrace the courage of the lone wolf, to energetically leave the expectations and conditions of her childhood behind to go forth and create a new way of living that was right and supportive for her.

We worked together to affirm my client's boundaries. There is an activity I conduct with my clients where we check in and feel the energy, feel, texture and proximity of one's boundaries. During this activity my client was shocked to find that she couldn't feel any. When we brought thoughts of her mother into the space, she found it difficult to discern as to where she ended and her mother began.

So, like the lone wolf she had to begin exploring new territories and establishing her own boundaries around the territory she wanted to create. She needed and utilised her inner masculine to bring discipline to this exploration and application and her inner feminine to intuitively decide what was right for her. The most powerful boundary for her was to say no. I gave her a grounding and protection practice to use once she was at her mothers, so her energy remained hers and only hers and so that from a grounded, centred place she could say to her mum when enough, was enough.

It did take practice and time for her mum to respect her wishes, but her mum eventually learnt the new boundaries and because they remained clear and sourced from a place of integrity, her mum came to honour them. My client found that she lost some extra pounds she had been carrying but more importantly she came to feel more at home in her body. She was listening to when it wanted to be fed and how, and honoured it. In doing so she established a relationship of trust with her herself and her body. The recipe book also become a special occasion, not a daily go to. She found a way to adapt its use, rather than fully rejecting it. It became instead a resource for when my client was entertaining, so she could share the large portions with her own wolf pack of friends. A bonus of this was that she had wonderful feedback to share with her mother of how much others had loved her food!

The reality for wolves in the wild is that most of their cleverness is channelled into survival. A wolf will not take unnecessary risks such as trying to fight or kill another as it knows it may be killed itself. The wolf cleverly discerns which conflict or prey is worth the effort as well as which location and which partners would be most beneficial for breeding.

Humans have the same survival instincts as animals and often we make choices that keep us small, limited, withheld, just because those same choices also bring perceived safety or continuity. Sometimes, however, being wolf means taking that courageous step outside of all that it known and understood and exploring and creating new ways of being. It does not always mean leaving our pack completely behind or abandoning all that we have loved or been taught but it does mean following your instinct about what is right for you and fearlessly pursing and embodying your own unique truth. So, how can we use the same Wolf discernment and utilising of the inner wisdom and knowing, in our own lives, so that we are thriving rather than just surviving?

Remember that every wolf within the pack is unique and individual, from the marking on their fur, to the way they hunt and the way they howl. Wolves fulfil their role within the pack, not through force or coercion but with a mutual goal and intention of harmony and united success. In their own time wolf matures and in their own way every wolf contributes. It is the same for you.

When you reflect on all of the roles and pack dynamics in your human life it is important to always remember that your body is yours, your life is yours, your voice and your choices, are yours. It is a balance that needs work sometimes, establishing and sustaining who you are within a family of birth and the family of society. Again and again, we may need to come back to what it means to be us at any given place or time in our lives. This can be especially relevant when we have changed role, or are leaving or finding a new one.

I invite you to spend some time now journalling, reflecting or creating art on the following:

1. What roles do you fulfil in your life? Daughter, son, mother, father or grandparent, friend, job, carer, leader,

boss or trainee? Right a little about each: what you do, how it feels, what it means to you, what it requires you to be. How did you grow into, resist or find rightness in these different roles?

2. Can you think of a time in your life when a role felt completely right and lit you up? Can you think of a time when you felt uncomfortable in a role, like it just didn't fit?
3. Are there any reoccurring or repeating themes, lessons, or insights? What can you learn about yourself in each role that hints at your core or essence of self?
4. What is that thread that runs through them all, the ingredients that make you, you? Perhaps list or draw two to five characteristics or strengths that you embody or demonstrate in every or most of your roles or positions in life. *Examples, active listener, creative, honest, self-motivated, kind, patient, passionate, open-minded, determined.*

   What are the skills or gifts that you uniquely have to offer?
5. Imagine or visualise yourself outside of all of your positions and titles. As if you were alone in a forest with no jobs or tasks to do an no obligations or conditions.

   Who are you, when it is just you, without the labels, the roles, the jobs and without the expectations, conditions or obligations? What is your essential self? What does it look like, feel like, or want to say or do?

THE CALL OF THE WOLF

That night the wind was howling almost like a wolf and there were some real wolves off to the west giving it lessons.
– George R.R. Martin

One of the most well-known characteristics of the wolf, is their call. There is something bone-tingling awe inspiring to hear wolves' howl. It speaks to our imagination, hearts and souls and brings forth a deep ancestral remembrance and stirring of root energy.

Just like us, every wolf has their own unique voice and can be recognised as such by each wolf and human that hears it. It is made individual through tone, pitch, intent, emotions, experience, context as well as the wolf's physicality. In the pack each wolf will instantly know which family member is calling and also be able to recognise when it is the voice of an unknown. They do not just hear a howl, growl or whimper, but know it, feel it, experience it. They know from the tone what that other wolf is trying to express, what they want from the type of call used and by pitch they will know the desire or the well-being of the other wolf. They know without asking whether their wolf family needs affectionate play, time alone, help or food.

This is all possible for us humans as well. Wolf reminds you that no one has your voice or your way of expressing, what you share is your unique perspective and creation. We should be encouraged as well to learn the nuances of those around us. A tone used by ourselves may have different intent or be received differently when used by another, a whisper can be one of fear, play, awe, shock, lust or gentleness depending on how or why it is used. What is your father, sister, lover, friend, boss truly asking for or wanting to share when they use those words or that tone? Are there more clues of intent and need in the depths of communication that lies even beyond the words?

There is much insight that we can gain from the call of the wolf. Just like we whisper, shout and mumble, wolves also have different sounds that they use. In fact, scientists have found that there are at least twenty-one different types of howls that wolves use and this verbal expression is just one form of their communication! Using a sound, a noise level or vibration wolves clearly express what it is they seek, want, desire or feel. Each call is also supported by the use of clear and expressive body language. Their vast effective and affective practices of communication remind us of the intent of our own communication; why are you saying what you are saying and how? What does it truly mean to say something softly, gently and what is the intention or effect of a shout? We know the result of a bark before we snap, so why do we do it?

So let us explore four different calls of the wolf; the bark, growl, whimper and howl. Then we shall reflect on what codes of wisdom and healing these calls offer us.

Bark

The bark of a wolf is either offensive or defensive. Many barks are to warn other members of the pack of incoming predators or threats. The bark can also be to call another wolf into a challenge, perhaps over territory. It can alternatively be used to incite a play fight or to test family pack members, and in learning about boundaries, much like the child that shouts 'mum, mum, mum' on repeat.

Growl

When a growl is lower pitched it signals dominance of that wolf over the wolf or animal it is growling at. It can act as a warning of impending confrontation.

A wolf may also growl when they are feeling threatened or unsafe.

Whimper

The whimper is for calmer situations than the bark or growl. A high-pitched whimper can indicate submission.

Wolves may also whimper as a friendly greeting to each other or sign of affection. Parents and pups may also speak to each other in general whimpers and mother wolf will use gentle whimpers to communicate with her new-borns, encouraging them with her soft voice and nurturing licks.

Howl

The Howl with his high pitch and suspension of notes can be a form of long distant communication between the pack. A howl of a wolf can actually reach as far as six miles in a forest and ten miles across clear land. The reason for the wolf lifting their noses up to the sky is actually all about the acoustics. The tilting of their heads allowing the projection of their calls upward so that the howl can travel further.

Different howls serve alternatively as a fire alarm, a rallying cry for the pack to meet up, a GPS signal to let the pack know where a wolf is, a warning for outside wolves to stay out of pack territory, and also fun family sing-alongs. Often wolves can be found sing-howling to themselves or other pack members just for the sheer fun and joy if it! Chorus howls are common and are when the pack howls in unison. Members will sing together but at multiple pitches and can use up to twelve different harmonies at a time to create their music.

Alpha males will usually also use a lower pitched howl and male wolves sometimes actually howl more frequently than other members of the pack. Imagine the male wolves all competing over who has the lowest growl or biggest howl, the pups playfully imitating the noises, while the she-wolves sit watching and rolling their eyes.

The howl can also be the sound of love! It is a sound heard more frequently during the autumn and early wintertime breeding season. At this time wolves seek out mates and are establishing the location of new or old packs. The howl can be used find out who is where and who is welcome. It is used when communicating with mates, with males making deeper tones, with the purpose of coming across as more attractive to the females. The whimper is used by both when they are in closer quarters.

The wolf whistle between humans derives its name from the call of the male wolf to his mate. The she-wolf chooses to whom she responds. She may hear many males calling and receive many requests but ultimately the she-wolf does not respond until she has chosen what is best for herself and her potential pack.

Lone wolves, may, however, not howl as much or as loudly as wolves in a pack or those that have found or are searching for their mate. For reasons of safety, they may want to keep their location hidden as they roam through different alien territories. With not having the protection of the pack this can help them with keeping hidden from potential threats.

As you can see there are so many different ways to communicate and reasons why a wolf would communicate. I cannot guarantee the effectiveness of howling at other humans we find attractive at the supermarket, however, there is much we can be reminded of in exploring the diversity of wolf communication!

What do we create?

Our voice is a powerful tool. Our words create, not just the words themselves, but also energy, emotion, memories, contraction, expansion, creation and destruction.

Let us use our internal dialogue or self-talk as an example.

When we talk to a baby or a child we talk tenderly and softly, with the hope they feel safe and loved. What if we also spoke to our own inner self/child in this way, rather than admonishing or shutting them down? Imagine if you shouted loudly every time baby had just fallen asleep! I imagine most people would say 'never!' but how often do we actually do this to ourselves.

We shout at the tender, vulnerable and perhaps softer, innocent parts of ourselves when actually what we truly need is some understanding and acceptance.

Awareness is the first step. With a baby we became acutely aware of the volume of our speech, we recognise the need for gentleness and adjust the words and volume used as needed. Become attuned to yourself in the same way and take notice of the form of your internal and external expression. When you speak, or think, harshly or loudly to yourself, really be curious about what affect that is creating. *Why* did you say it or feel it? What triggered it? What need within yourself is calling for attention? Perhaps even what habit or imprint from another are you repeating? With a baby you would want to know *why* it was crying or screaming and so seek to discover your own whys.

The next step is to then do a kindness to yourself and choose to create communion with self that has compassionate intentions. Even if you can't speak lovingly yet, start with compassionately and patiently. Give yourself time and space, be honest, but without critical judgement. Take small steps and show up with wolf determination and stamina. Maybe even ask for support from Wolf in accessing and embodying courage and consistency. Be open to a deepening awareness of what it is that you are choosing to create with your tone and words.

What would it create for you if you approached and spoke to your own body and self as you do to your lover or your child? What if you offered yourself words of celebration, a tone of encouragement and tenderness rather than the barking that is it wrong, stupid or a hindrance? How would that feel?

Do a kindness to others as well by offering the same compassion and consideration to forms of communication that you choose or use. Why do you always shout at *that* person? What makes you express with quiet or confidence in a certain situation? What is revealed in your forms of communication?

What within you wants to make itself known, healed, acknowledged or explored?

Remember that breath is also deeply connected to speech; air and communication can both enter and leave via our mouth and nose, breath and words fuse together in our hearts and via our blood they travel in unison throughout our body, from our toes to our brain, to our lungs and then exit together to create, move, dissipate or transform. Try breathing deeply with your thoughts and try breathing with your whole body as you form and create any kind of expression. Try deeply breathing with your words, feel your words in your toes, your belly, your bones and consciously be present, giving words the depth and fullness of time and space, they deserve.

Compassion for our journey

For many, myself including, the authenticity and sound of their voice is something that can be a lifelong journey in reclaiming. There may have been or you may still be in a time in your life when you fear, mistrust, doubt or hide your voice. Some of you may feel like the lone wolf that keeps quiet so as not to be seen or heard. Or you may feel like a threatened wolf whose barks at any other that comes near its territory. Actively working with the lessons of the wolves or embodying wolf essence and energy can help you to reclaim your voice. Wolves as an example, or as archetype, can offer a pathway to work on sounding and exploring your unique expression.

So, what is it that wolf pups do to learn how to howl? Practice, practice, practice!

Ok maybe it didn't work barking in *that* particular situation, does it therefore need a whimper? Do you need to utilise a howl of your boundaries or desires *before* the need for it to be barked? Or have you found that in certain situations time to be quiet and listen is most effective?

Have compassion, understanding and allowance for yourself when you are practising to howl, whimper, growl or bark in human tones. Through practice you *will* find your own voice and way of speaking and you will learn not only how to communicate truthfully and effectively, but also when, why and what to speak. Create a beginning for yourself by taking some action, whether that be reflecting, journalling and writing, speaking more or speaking different. This is the only place you can start, even the wolves aren't born knowing, we all must learn and develop ways to reach each other authentically and effectively.

I invite you to journal and reflect on these questions. Approach with honesty, curiosity and without judgement

1. Which form of communication do you favour, or have you utilised most in life?
   For example, do you find that you bark a lot, or do you always default to a whimper and feel its stems from shyness or low confidence?
2. In your life what communication has been supportive or easeful and which has been more difficult or harmful? (To yourself or others.)
3. Has there been a pivotal or stand out time or experience when you have learnt something about the way you did, do or could communicate?
4. Is there any area or type of communication that calls for more practice? How or what could you practice?
5. What do you fear or worry would happen if you communicated your true needs or desires?
6. How, why or when do you feel your voice has been shut down?
7. What steps can you take to empower and express your unique and authentic voice now?

Client example of communication teachings and healings.

I had a client that chose to work with me because she wanted answers as to why it seemed that to her everything in her life kept 'failing'. She thought she was unlucky because often events, classes or occasions she attended would end up finishing and she felt like it was her fault. She was confused as to why people often got angry with her or snapped at her and conversations with others felt like battlegrounds.

Coming to me was the first time she had asked for help! We began with acknowledging that, her true wolf courage in choosing a path of finding answers and her bravery in being honest with herself that perhaps there was something she could do to create change.

Self-responsibility really is a game changer!

I found that during sessions with this client the way she talked was almost like a continuous bark. She would snap and criticise everyone and everything in her life, from her partner, her parents, to her gym instructor. What was revealed was that she had a habit of finding reasons for conflict, creating scenarios in her head and in her reality that would lead to arguments or tension.

Through our sessions together I could feel that she was full of unexpressed anger and resentment and that it would leak out into her speech and communication, almost like an overboiling pot. We explored this and through working together, we discovered a link between the healing that was needed at her throat chakra to an unresolved wounding within her heart. It turned out that her harsh forms of communication ultimately had its roots in unexpressed grief. She would use her words as attempts to trigger people. In triggering people, she was hoping for conflict or anger which would re-enforce her feelings of being the victim and of being hurt. She knew hurt, she knew pain and she had to keep it because what was her life without it?

The lady had lost her only child in a horrific accident a decade before. To my client I was to blame, her partner was to blame, her gym instructor, the till operator at her supermarket, everyone was to blame. She wanted to shout and scream at us all, because we were alive and had not stopped her daughter from dying. However, she didn't shout and scream, she never had. She had filled the gap left by her daughter with anger and resentment. She closed down her throat to the expression it needed and it, as a result, continually clawed for her attention.

Her unexpressed grief manifested through into hateful speech and was pushing everyone away that could not only support her, but also love her. With the realisation and acknowledgement of all of this my client was able to begin creating space for her grief. I am so proud that she chose to explore and express her grief finally, it was a huge and brave step! We created sacred space and activities for her to give unrestrained, unlimited, unconditional expression and release from her throat chakra. She needed tears, screams, she needed to be untamed and wild for a time.

With the courage of wolf, she gave herself the sacred time to be angry, to be in the emotions and feelings that she had thought would rip her apart.

In a safe, and supported space, she chose not to 'hold herself together', to not be ok, to rage at life, at fate, at her daughter for dying, at God for taking her and for all those still alive. She learnt that it wasn't wrong to give voice to her true emotions and feelings, but that there is a healthy time and a place for grief and anger. She discovered that barking at everyone she met and creating conflict was an unhealthy way of dealing with suppressed emotion but that there were other ways, supportive and appropriate for her, that would make resolution and healing possible. She also found that her anger could be channelled and transformed into power and strength and eventually set up a charity to support awareness around women and alcoholism.

It took time and devotion to healing but my client finally came to a place where she felt she could draw a line. Having given the time and space to expressing her grief, rage and anger, she felt able to move on from it and separate it as the before, so she could move into the after.

Sometimes we are not aware of what we create with our words. Other times perhaps we do have an awareness and are left with feelings of shame, guilt or remorse. Your communication is powerful, whether you chose to embrace that or reject it. Your voice is the vehicle through which you express yourself, your intentions, your emotions, your needs and your hopes and I invite you to use self-awareness as a transformational tool. Instead of feeling guilty about snapping at someone, instead of being grumpy that you did so, ask why did I snap. With the curiosity of a five-year-old child who keeping asking why and why again, follow the breadcrumbs of those whys until you find a place of realisation and revelation. If your words and tone are a reflection of your inner realms, what do they reveal about what is present within you? Don't make your feelings or needs wrong, give them the gift of allowance and talk to them, reflect on them, learn from them. There are also any ways you can express without it coming through your voice! You can make music about it, draw or paint your feelings, you can journal to navigate through thoughts, you can dance with and or physically move your emotions or use movement to locate them. Remember don't repress but express, always! Just find the right way to do so for you at that time and ask for support when needed. I share some extra tools and practices for working with your throat chakra in Chapter 8 of this book.

Finally, next time you notice your own bark, howl, growl or whimper ask the essence of Wolf to support you in revealing what is being shown to you about the power of your language frequency. Ask Wolf for guidance around whether there is something to learn, discover, change or transform around your communication codes.

Reflections on working with the example of real wolves and what it means to embody

In later chapters of this book, we will discover that in spiritual and cultural archaeology and history we are presented with examples from the past of many wolf priests, shamans, tribes and deities. In them we see reflected the characteristics, themes and attributes of the physical wolf that I have shared in this chapter. An interesting aspect of the connection between these persons and the wolf is that the wolf shamans, priests, mascots or tribe leaders are often found depicted in, or described as wearing, a cloak of wolfskin.

This act of wearing the skin of their totem or sacred animal was the act of putting on the cloak of transformation, taking that person from one state to another. They are not just honouring the wolf, but by being surrounded by its skin, they *become* wolf. There is a change physically, emotionally and spiritually that occurs as one embodies, channels or emulates the spirit or essence of another. When you choose to embody or emulate the characteristics or wisdom of the wolf, you are also metaphorically putting on the wolf cloak.

The cloak holds the power, strength, wisdom and energy of the wolf and yet underneath we are human still. In the act of putting on the wolf skin cloak we do not loose ourself in other, but become more of ourselves. This is because with the aid of wolf, we discern and then choose those parts of ourselves that we wish to develop and grow. We move, speak and act as our human self but we intentionally place ourselves within the container of wolf to feel and emulate aspects of their being, whether that be courage or maternity.

And so, embodying the wolf means to uniquely witness those characteristics and attributes that they show us, learn from them and perhaps emulate them in a way that resonates or is uniquely true for you. To put on the wolf cloak of transformation will lead you to authentic expression and empowerment, rather than simple imitation.

As an example, one of the most celebrated characteristics of wolves is their courage. Yet courage means many different things for many people, including even the wolves themselves. For the wolf, courage is setting off as a lone wolf to seek a partner or fearlessly defending one's pack against another pack. For us humans, embodying a wolf's courage may mean for some just leaving the house one day despite feeling anxious or fearful. It may be trying a new food or for someone else it may be enforcing boundaries with an overbearing work colleague. It may also be going to the dentist, letting your hair be its natural grey, or it may be giving a TEDx talk to thousands of people.

To be wolf, is to be *your* unique courage.

Most of all, with embodiment, practice makes progress. No one is confident or capable overnight. When I was very young my throat chakra was so closed down it put me in danger. I was so scared to share or ask for what I wanted that there were times when I went without food, drink and the toilet for many, many hours. This majorly impacted my health and self-authority but due to a deep-seated fear of being told of and that I wanted to be a good girl, I waited for permission from someone else, in all things, rather than giving it to myself. I became conditioned into waiting for someone to tell me what to do, rather than thinking for myself. In my early teens, hiding in self-doubt became the safer option rather than speaking up for my needs and being seen. It wasn't till my mid-twenties that I begin to learn about the importance and power of self-fulfilment and self-responsibility. For me, the most courageous thing I could do was seeking and choosing self-care as an absolute priority, then claiming and using my voice on behalf of my well-being. Now, fully embodying my inner she-wolf I have a clear understanding and acknowledgement of my desires, needs and capabilities and I show up for myself. Self-care has become a devotional act, to the self that I love, honour and respect. Courage for me was using my voice to ask myself and others for what I truly needed. My healing journey was finding trust of my own inner knowing and confidently howling my authentic song.

How and when *you* put on the wolf skin cloak and embody wolf, will be completely unique to you. You will have already felt some particular resonance or inspiration from what has already been shared. What you felt deeply, or what triggered or intrigued you is your insight into the flavour of your wolf embodiment journey. Throughout this continued journey remember that your wolf guides and guardians will run with you towards yourself. While you run with the pack the human clothes of shame and fear of self will be stripped away from you till what is left is authentic and aligned with your divine essence.

They will invite you into embodiment that celebrates who and what you essentially are. They will remind you that you are as unique and precious as the trees, the wind, as gold, and that being made of the earth, you are sacred and holy. When you remember to honour your true self, you will find your sense of belonging and rightness not just as part of the human or wolf pack, but the pack of cosmos and creation. Wolves teach us that our food is our brother, that the elements are our pack members, that the earth is our alpha wolf, that the stars are the edge of the territory of our potentiality. You are an integral part of it all, so, like the wolf, play your part well.

Conclusion

Before we leave this chapter reflect back on all that you have learnt about wolf so far. I invite you to journal, paint, dance, mediate, talk or reflect on what the wolves can or have taught you about yourself and your unique journey and healing. Here are some questions that may support you in bringing a conclusion to this section of exploration.

1. What does it mean for you to embody wolf?
2. Do you already have some knowing about why you have been drawn to connect with the wolves? Did any memories, thoughts or triggers arise that can give you further insight about your journey?
3. What resonated most for you in this chapter? Did a pack role or lesson stand out to you?
4. What has wolf taught you about who or what you are?

Chapter 2

From Wild, Warrior Wolf to the Goddess's Lap Dog

We humans fear the beast within the wolf because we do not understand the beast within ourselves. – Gerald Hausman

Wolf has been prominent in iconography, religion, mythology and legend throughout human history. The wide and continuous use of both the image and idea of the wolf is testament to both their important connection to humankind and the effectiveness with which they can inspire and motivate feelings and ideas.

There is evidence to demonstrate that there have been close relations, rather than just co-existence, between wolf and human that goes back 100,000 years.[4] From the Upper Palaeolithic footprints of a wolf and child walking side by side in the Chauvet Cave in France, to a 1st century BCE. battle helmet with wolf decoration in Yugoslavia, we find many fascinating relics and artefacts both in history and archaeology that demonstrate what wolf symbolised and meant for both our ancestors and the world that they lived in.

This chapter is an introduction to the meaning of wolf within European cultural and religious history. I will briefly cover the use of wolf as symbol and totem, as well as the use of the wolf as an idea or concept in folklore and tale. In doing so we will be able to witness what has been explored, believed and created in the past and from that come to our own viewpoints and choices, feeling into what most resonates and makes sense to you. All that I share here now points at the significance of wolf in history, yet it is also offered to you as a buffet of wolf occurrences from which you can be inspired to begin creating your own experience.

WOLF IN SYMBOLOGY, FOLKLORE AND CULTURAL ICONOGRAPHY

When we choose a symbol, for ourselves, our tribe, family or even country, we do so because there is something about that symbol that we feel represents either our character or our personality as it is, or how we wish it to be. The face, body, teeth and skin of wolves were all used as symbol and icon in historic Europe and it is where, how and why these depictions were used that hint at what the people of the past thought of wolf and its character or even in some cases of its magical powers.

Let us begin with Ancient Greece and how the image of wolf there was associated with both folktale and superstitious belief. One example is that the ancient Greeks believed that a wolf spectre had the power to make people lose their speech with its stare alone. It is possible that this was a hint at the believed power of the wolf to cast speechlessness upon its victim, or that the speechlessness was believed to be caused from sheer terror of the ghostly apparition. It does demonstrate the perspective that the ancient Greeks had of wolves, that they were something to be feared as possibly unpleasant or dangerous. This viewpoint is perhaps also hinted in the well-known legend of King Lycaon, one of the most ancient kings of Arcadia. He was turned into a wolf by the Great God Zeus as a punishment for deception and in this tale, it is Lycaon's lies are that which cause his punishment. Knowing what we have explored already in regards to the connection with wolves and healing communication and expression, perhaps wise and almighty Zeus changed Lycaon into a wolf to learn how to speak truth. As Lycaon ordered the murder of his child as part of his deception becoming a Wolf was also a suitable experience to learn wolf's ferocious protection, nurturance and guardianship that they show towards their own pups. One can only hope that he emerged from his experience a less self-centred father!

However, it could also be argued that this legend to the ancient Greeks was primarily important as a deterrent, encouraging those who heard the tale to not deceive or disobey the gods. Possibly living in the body of a wild and untamed creature that was loyal to its animal instincts was deemed by the intellectual Greeks as a most terrifying prospect. One lasting mark was also made on the original landscape of this legend. The mountain of the sacrifice and transformation became known as Mount Lycaeus or Lykaion, Wolf Mountain. It still has this name today highlighting how the impact of wolf stories can still be witnessed even many thousands of years after.

The power of the wolf was also referenced not just in legends but also in physical objects that played an important part in ritual or ceremony. In Yarmouth, UK, a Roman bronze wolf was found by archaeologists, that was designed to be mounted on the top of an Iron Age religious staff. The staff was used in the Iron Age period as an emblem of power and a reference to the ability and willpower to make change. Therefore, this depiction in this context is a reminder, to both the user and the observer, of the wolf as a symbol of strength and leadership. It is a nod to the unquestionable authority of the man that held it, who would have reflected or embodied the mighty and potentially deadly wolf. Interestingly the wolf was also used as a symbol or mascot by the leadership by the Iron age tribes of Northern England called the Brigantes. They were noted for their formidable female leadership and some historians have claimed they were also worshippers of an early form of Brigid, a Goddess who herself has a wolf companion or totem.

Just outside of Europe the wolf was also connected to leaders and the power and authority they were expected to emulate and personify. In ancient Egypt Upuaut (or Wep-wawet) was a wolf god whose standard accompanied the Pharoah into battle and whose name meant 'he who opens up ways and paths'. His standard would have been seen and known by the adversaries of Egypt in battle and associated with the Egyptian army. However, he most specifically with the warrior pharaoh, hinting at the Pharaoh's wolf like attributes but would also accompany the Pharoah on hunts as a scout and play a part in royal rituals. This association with power and authority both in battle and leadership is very similar to the Roman God Mars who was one of the chosen patrons of both army and emperor and symbolised by a black wolf. Here is a great example of the repeated allegory of the wolf as fearless warrior, who like the predatory wolf to its prey, will bring death and destruction.

As well as a symbol of leadership and even kingship, the wolf was also represented in historic Europe as a magical being, connected to and sometimes even the companion of not just kings but also heroes and mystical figures.

In Russian folktale the wolf is portrayed as guide and advisor in story Prince Ivan and the Firebird. In the fairy tale a magical grey wolf helps Prince Ivan to find the firebird, so that he may take it to his father the king, become his heir and gain half of his kingdom. The wolf plays a pivotal part in restoring life through magical waters and also acts as Ivan's steed. The grey wolf not only carries him but advises and guides Ivan throughout his journey.

The Volva (meaning Germanic seeress or prophetess) Hyndla also rides a wolf in her legend, as it carries her to Valhalla, with the Goddess Freyja her companion riding a boar. The wolf acts here as a vehicle to journey from one place, or dimension to another. Along with the pig, the wolf was also one of the magical creatures that protected and guarded the great bard and high druid Merlin. The wolf in particular is noted as also offering Merlin companionship. In Celtic folktale pig and wolf, especially of white variety, are connected through their both being guides to, and guardians of, the otherworld.

It is not unusual to find the wolf as companion. In the Irish folktale of the character Suibhne Geilt, he spends some winters living and hunting with wolves during his wandering years. He gains the title Madman but is inspired while in his 'madness' and composes celebrated verse during his time in the wild. In all instances of Merlin, Geilt, Ivan and Hyndla the wolf plays a significant part, as their guardian and guide, during a journey of transition, transformation or enlightenment.

Another mythological being or person that was associated with wolves was Ragana who was an enchantress or witch from Latvian and Lithuanian mythology. She was known for her ability to transform humans into animals and in particular she was often inclined to turn men into wolves or dogs. In similar stories to that of Circe in Greek Mythology with pigs, the turning of a man into a wolf serves to teach him a lesson or a punishment for his misdeeds. In becoming a wolf, he perhaps receives insight or guidance on the conduct in his past and future paths or he learns something only to be gained through the experience of being a wolf. Alternatively, it could have been seen as a punishment to lose human free will and become wild without restraint.

To take the form of a wolf, was also used as a punishment for those that had conducted misdeeds in Celtic myth. Gwydion and Gilfaethwy from Welsh Mythology are turned into various animals, including a wolf and she-wolf as punishment for various crimes, including rape. The punishment serves as a morality lesson. When one has had to live in the body of an animal, without choice when it comes to responding to needs and desires, it serves as a hard reminder that it is humans alone that can comprehend and then choose between right and wrong. They are reminded that with free will comes responsibility. The animals they are turned into pig, deer and wolf, are three of the most sacred of ancient animals, linked to the divine and nobility or kingship, and obviously chosen with specific lessons in mind that would be different than that of being say turned into a worm or fish.

Wolf was also in some cultures considered to be connected to the wild and deemed to be the guardians of wild places, such as woods, forests and mountains. An example is the tales of wolves from the area around Laskowice, Poland. Here Slavic Forest spirits were particularly connected with the wolves and were considered to protect other wild animals in the forests. Rituals and dance were thought to have been enacted by wise men or actors who ritually put on the pelt of a wolf to assimilate with the essence or spirit of the animal. They would literally become wolf, transforming into the animal through taking on its skin as a cloak, with the cloak being a barrier and a doorway to that beyond the human realm. Vlkodlak was a Slavic wolf man from folklore, who represented the ancient respect accorded to the ravenous wolf, an animal who was one of the most feared in northern and eastern Europe. And in Serbia the Wolf was also considered a totem, representing fearlessness and protection. Again, there is evidence here for wolf skin rituals being used as part of an initiation or spiritual experience. Archaeologists can only speculate that it was a way of channelling or embodying the energy of the wolf, but whether magical companion, revered spirit or an inspirer of fear, the popularity of the wolf as a symbol to connect with or emulate is in itself undisputable.

Wolf has also proved popular as a tribal or group emblem. In heraldic symbolism the wolf stood for perseverance and dedication, as well as noble courage. When the wolf is used as a symbol on a shield specifically it was used for protection from harm but also a personal emblem, identifying the user as either protected by the wolf, or having the characteristics of a wolf.

In another heraldic depiction of wolf, Neubecker shares an Italian heraldic design on a coin which shows a wolf standing over a lamb it has presumably bitten.[5] It is accompanied by the motto "what happens through mercy" referring to the mercy of death. The wolf in this context therefore symbolises the power of death and endings, and in this context the ability of the owner to inflict this death or the intimidating might of the user that makes their enemy long for death.

In Passau, Germany, a red wolf rampant is used as the emblem for their city and state heraldry. In this case the wolf stands for valour and guardianship. The red of the wolf matches the wolf own themes, with this specific colour symbolising generosity, as well as warrior strength and or martyrdom.

Chirk Castle Gate with the Myddelton Wolves in statue and on the shield. Wales.

Chirk Castle in Wales also has the wolf as its emblem and heraldry in reference to the Welsh wolf ancestry of the castle owners. Wolves can still be seen as statues on the estate gates and as building decoration. The wolf depictions are standing guard as a reminder of the families' wolf ancestry, just as once the family kept lives wolves in the gatehouse of the castle in pride and remembrance of the castle's past. The famous wolf ancestors were, Rhirid Flaidd 'The Wolf' and Blaidd Rhudd 'The Bloody Wolf'. They were Welsh lords of the early Medieval period. Their connection to Wolves was through a fierce character displayed in their defence of their Welsh homeland from English invaders. The motto that accompanied this heraldry is 'In Veritate Triumpho' *I triumph in truth'* hinting at themes of authenticity, justice and recompense, where falsehood will be defeated.

This is also an example of how animals could become a symbol of home, inheritance and personal identity. The Chirk Castle example is similar in this to the she-wolf Lupa becoming the symbol of Rome and the Ancient Romans. Lupa was the she-wolf who famously rescued and suckled the founders of Rome, Romulus and Remus and in doing so pivoted the course of history towards the creation of one of Europe's greatest empires. The she-wolf became a symbol and remembrance of origin for the Roman people under her banner and instilled a sense of pride and place. In both context's the wolf symbolised the qualities and characteristics that had become important for the people to connect with and emulate but also a vital link to their past and ancestors.

In a similar way in traditional Christian and Jewish iconography, the Wolf was the symbol of the Tribe of Benjamin. In the Old Testament Benjamin was the youngest son, and known as the right hand, of Jacob. He was also the son of the holy bloodline and sacred womb of Rachel, believed by some to be a priestess of Inanna. His tribe became known as the ravenous wolf, distinguished for their courage, military might and cleverness. Their territory included the holy lands of Jerusalem and he was the founding father of the Israelite tribe of Benjamin. Some claim that this royal blood line was still signified with the use of the wolf symbol and heraldry by his nomadic descendants who found their way into Nordic lands. Like wolves who sometimes travel great distances to establish new territories and packs, the wolf in this context may have also been a signifier of the destiny of this tribe, a fatalistic reference to the nomadic and future vast reach of these people.

The Hebrews had left the Mesopotamian city of Ur and became wandering herders where they then begin the lineage of Abraham, to his son Isaac, and from Isaac to Jacob. So, from the guardian wolf of the Mesopotamian Great Goddess Ishtar (also Sumerian Inanna), we can perhaps follow a wolf lineage that is carried down through the wolf tribe of Benjamin to his descendants that became the Norsemen of Nordic lands. In Norse mythology wolves were considered the hounds of the Norns. These wolves were the companions of these female beings, sometimes considered deities, who also played a part in the shaping of the course of human destiny. The norms would sit at the foot of the tree, Yggdrasil, spinning the threads of fate, while the wolves guarded and protected. The presence of wolves in association with the idea of fate and destiny is again much like the presence of the She-Wolf Lupa steering the fate of Romulus and Remus, as well as the destiny of wolf tribe of Benjamin who would reach the farthest and widest of the tribes of Jacob.

The presence of a wolf in tales and beliefs of destiny or fate often then indicated or hinted of a people, person, tribe or idea that will triumph, perhaps over all else and would share similar characteristics of endurance, determination and might as the wolf.

The same tenacity may well have been referenced in the case of the wolf in medieval Europe also being associated with outlaws. Outlaws were considered much like the lone-wolves who have left the pack. They lived on the outskirts of society and were independent of the laws and rules of the land or 'pack'.

Fulk Fitzwarin III, outlaw, medieval lord and inspiration for the legend of Robin Hood, was described as and given the epithet 'The Wolf'. He was immortalised in legend along with his wolfish band of outlaws. In open rebellion to King John, he was a danger to all those that kept in line and kept quiet. It was quite a concern that the wolf may lead the innocent and conforming, deep into the wood and teach them his untamed ways. This idea is further emphasised by the term sheep, the traditional prey of the wolf, being used for those that follow without conscious choice or full awareness. For the sheep to follow, not only relies on the naivety of the sheep, but also assumes the cleverness or persuasive powers of the wolf.

The wolf, could be used as a very personal totem as well as being the symbol for an idea, group or people. An example of this more personal use of the wolf by our ancestors is the talisman. Headdresses, necklaces and other personal ornament made of animal's teeth may have had spiritual meaning and use as far back at the stone age people. The wearers of these talismans, that have been found in archaeology as well as portrayed in art, may have believed that the teeth held the characteristics or energy of the animal from which they came from. Such an example is the ornamental wolf teeth pendant or amulet found next to a skeleton at Hallstatt, an Iron Age site in Austria. We can never know what this symbol meant to the human who chose it as their personal ornament, but it was well worn and they kept it close to their chest and heart, even into death. There is also written evidence that wolf talismans were used in other countries such as Slovenia and Italy. In the case of ancient Rome, the wolf talisman was noted to be a form of protection against evil.

I share in my book Lupa that:

> *Pliny, a respected Roman writer, also noted the belief that was still held by the Romans in the 1st century AD, that if an amulet of a wolf's tooth was worn by children it would protect them from nightmares.*[6]

There are other occurrences of wolf deposits in burial sites. Archaeologists speculate on some sort of wolf ritual being involved with the pre-Iron age remains that were discovered at the Škocjan Caves, in Slovenia. The parts of at least fifteen wolves were discovered in a deposit, along with eleven human skeletons and three dogs. Interestingly it was the skulls and teeth alone that remained of the wolves, with no other body parts being in evidence in the caves It does seem that from evidence of archaeological sites that the remains of wolves are very rarely discovered within the context of human burial, but are actually more often found in ceremonial or ritual areas like the Škocjan Caves.

Remains of the image of the wolf is even more frequent than parts of the actual wolf itself. I beautiful example of this is the sounding head of a horn in the form of a snarling wolf's head from an ancient Celtiberian settlement in Spain. In sharing about this object, Miranda Green suggests that although the images of wolf seen to be prolific, there is also little evidence that they were actually hunted.[7] She goes on to suggest that rather being considered prey, wolves may be one of those animals whose small number of bone present in burials, pits and settlement remains was only due to use of their fur and their involvement in ritual and or ceremony. This supports the idea that archaeologists speculated at the Slovenian caves that the remains, image and perhaps even the idea of the wolf was connected in some way to the spiritual beliefs of our ancestors more than so than having an everyday presence or practical use in human life.

Reinforcing the idea of a connection between wolf and ritual, Marija Gimbutas shares that there is much evidence to connect the wolf with initiation practices of Indo-European cultures. She explains a running theme of male youths forming a band and living together in wild places as an initiation time to mark the threshold moment between childhood and manhood. In the depictions of these initiations the wolf is shown facing or accompanying the youths and the name 'wolf-band' was also given to these groups.[8] This is similar in a way to the traditions of the Roman Lupercalia festival during which it was young men who imitated the run of Romulus, circling Rome from the cave of Lupa and back. A certain wildness or freedom was offered during this rite of remembrance. It recreated the sacred transformation of Romulus and Remus from babes to kings, and of Rome from hut to city, under the guardianship of goddess Lupa. All those that took part in the ritual were initiated as a son of the She-Wolf.[9]

GOOD OR BAD WOLF?

In all the examples explored so far of wolf as totem, symbol and mascot, we have already had a glimpse of the diverse points of connection to wolf. Some of these connections hint at viewpoints that are almost polar opposite; good or bad, deadly or saviour. We find the term and idea of wolf used in so many different ways that have both negative and positive connotations. This again displays the way that wolf embodies paradox and that the power of wolf lies in that it can mean very different things for different people and be called on as a guide and ally for a huge range of reasons.

It seems that one way in which this polar opposition seems to have been created is merely through our gradual detachment over time from nature and our nature. The wolf may have been revered or important in a positive way to our most ancient ancestors, as shown by the deposits and images in both ritual items and burial deposits. However, we find that later in the Middle Ages of Europe the wolf came to represent evil. This later viewpoint was propaganda, spread due to the wolf's wildness and inability to be tamed and obedient, it was a useful metaphor for the wildness within that came to be feared and shameful. Yet the wolf as evil may also have grown from genuine fear of the vulnerability of precious livestock to any predator, whether human or wolf. To bring the wolf, both external in the forest and internal within self, into confinement and strict compliance became something to be celebrated in the medieval period. St David and St. Francis were just two of a few saints of whom it was written were able to tame the dangerous wolf and exert their authority over animals on behalf of God. An animal that was once respected or revered became something to oppress or control because of the fear of potentiality and freedom.

In Norse mythology the wolf also has both negative and positive connotations. Fenrir, the wolf and son of the Loki is considered so dangerous that he must be bound by the gods. Fenrir was also fated to consume the God Odin at the end of days, while Fenrir's children, Sköll and Hati, would consume the sun and moon, together bringing complete destruction to existence, before its eventual renewal. However, Odin himself has two 'good' wolves as his companions, Grei and Freki and unlike Fenrir, they were deemed safe, having learnt obedience and were considered his faithful pets. In this context whether the wolf is good or bad is determined by its submission or threat to, the Senior God, Odin. Must like the legend of Lycaon I shared previously, loyalty to an authority, whether king or God, was rewarded and disobedience punished. The good wolf at heel representing the loyal and the wild, untamed, dangerous wolf representing the unruly.

If we take Ancient Rome as another example, here we also find contrasting viewpoints on wolf. We need only look to prostitutes and warriors to discover how the label wolf can reflect societal judgements and cultural dogmas.

The She-Wolf in ancient Rome referenced two very different situations. Firstly, there was the She-Wolf herself, the rescuer, guardian and milk mother of Romulus and Remus, the founders of Rome. Her name was Lupa, deified as Goddess Luperca and she was honoured, celebrated and recognised for her essential involvement in the foundation of the city of Rome. She was the divine intervention that saved Romulus and Remus as babes, from drowning in the river, feeding through her breastmilk and then initiating them into kingship in her sacred cave. In this context Lupa meant ferocious protection and nurturing care. She was celebrated, honoured and essentially 'good', working on behalf of humankind.

However, the term Lupa in Ancient Rome also meant prostitute. In a profound example of the paradox of wolf, while the She-Wolf deity herself was celebrated for her ferocity, at the same time the assumed characteristics in some women of Rome were condemned. What was celebrated in the divine feminine was not celebrated in her human manifestations. What we see with the prostitutes of Rome is an equation of certain 'negative' female attributes with those of a wild and predatory animal.

I share in my book *Lupa*, that:

The word Lupa was most often used in slang to mean a low-level prostitute and a Lupanar, meaning wolf's den, to mean a lower-class brothel. However, in ancient Pompeii the biggest, best planned and most richly decorated brothel is also known as the Lupanarium, meaning 'the wolves lair'. The term Lupa was given in reference to the belief in the prostitute's predatory nature, who would actively ensnare their clients, like a lamb hunted by a wolf.[10]

In later Medieval England we also have many European queens that are given the title 'She-Wolf' as a derogatory term, hinting at the widely held opinion of the time that a woman in power could be deadly. The She-Wolf Queens such as Matilda, Eleanor of Aquitaine, Isabella of France and Margaret of Anjou were those that were assertive, or attempted to carve their own path, or honour their own needs or desires, rather than submitting to the higher authority of men, or retreating to a passive role of broodmare.

While the term she-wolf sometimes had negative associations or characteristics that where not celebrated in a woman, the same attributes were celebrated in men.

Frenzy warriors wearing the skins of wolves called Ulfheðnar in Norse sagas were said to take on or embody the energy, spirit, or characteristics of the wolf. They were celebrated and admired for their ruthlessness, exceptional fearlessness, strength and self-control that went well beyond the scope of the normal warrior.

The Wolf and its characteristics also had very positive connotations for Roman men. They were encouraged to emulate or embody the deadly and brave fighting skills of the wolf. Roman warriors used the God Mars' Wolf as their emblem and we celebrated for their wolf ferocity and fearlessness in battle. A few Roman Emperors, most notably Julius Caesar and Emperor Augustus. also claimed their descent from the founding father and wolf king Romulus as a hint to their having the same divine favour and wolf characteristics.

Despite the fact that the wolf had negative associations for women and positive associations for men, in honour and remembrance of Mars, Romulus and the Goddess Lupa, all Roman citizens, men, women and children, did identify themselves with the symbol of the wolf and it came to a mascot for the whole empire.

Similar to the Wolf warriors of Mars, in Germanic tribes the wolf was also one of three 'beasts of battle' along with the raven and the eagle. They believed in the insatiable hungry wolf that would devour the bodies of the dead on the battlefield, though whether this was witnessed or merely believed in, we cannot be sure. In this way the wolf was not the killer in battle as man was, but actually the vehicle through which the body was transformed and transmuted after death. The dead body through being devoured by this threshold creature could in this context also serve as a sacrifice; a sacrifice to a symbolic creature of the wild and untamed earth, in a nod to the necessity, honour or eventuality of death.

So, like death, the wolf whether good or bad, was considered necessary and an inevitable part of nature. This predator, though perhaps feared, was an essential and respected part of the circle of life.

Wolf often reflects not only the different expectations and projections on each gender, but also reflects the limitations placed on identity and self-fulfilment caused by fear, discrimination or the need to control. There are still the labels of women as soft and emotional and men as strong and unfeeling, that both genders are confined and pressured by, just as wolf is deemed and treated as either solely good or evil.

Perhaps then the example of wolf offers a lesson on stereotyping and how limiting expectations or conditions can be. All of us humans can find definition and labels reassuring but at the same time there comes a point when placing a living, breathing animal, human or soul within an unmovable box of judgement only creates blame, fear and segregation.

We can also use labels to validate our own behaviour and judgements. How many times have you said, 'I'm sorry, but I only did that because I am just an angry/lazy/shy/assertive/kind person'? How many times have you expected or required that someone act or be a certain way because of the judgements you hold about their gender, age, race, class or background? How often can a stereotype become something to fall back on or excuse our behaviour rather than choosing to take self-responsibility or creating change for the better?

Are you a good or bad wolf?

Spend a moment before we move on to reflect on self-imposed or societal imposed labels.

Wolf has been bad, ugly, deadly, hero, saviour and kind. Many, past and present, have viewpoints on what wolf is and what it represents. Wolf is both killer of the livestock and protector of the livestock, it is deemed as either the aspect of the wild woman that longs to be liberated from patriarchal oppression, or the ultimate example of what a patriarchal man should be; strong, fearless, ruthless. Sure, it can be all these things, but wolf is not just these things. It is not just one or the other, either, or.

We must remember that Wolf is often what *we* choose it to be, whether that is because we relate to a certain aspect of wolf or because what we label it validates the judgements and expectations we have chosen or that have been chosen for us.

So how do we liberate wolf from the confines, limitations and expectations that we have created over time? We offer that liberation to ourselves.

Once you have experienced the freedom and the feeling of being seen, heard and acknowledged for what and who you truly are, not what others think we should be, you will want the same resulting joy and compassion to be experienced by all others, human and animal.

To be free, *you* must ultimately be the sole creator of your identity, choose only self-validation and permission and then seek belonging from a place of authenticity. No one will truly see you unless you reveal the real you. You will never fit, until you truthfully, honestly and compassionately know the you that is trying to fit. To find your place, to find your path, to find understanding from others, you must remember or accept the wolf that you are, raw, untamed and unfiltered. You belong within your own embrace first. You deserve to feel the joy of being naked, paw deep in earth, every scar, curve, wrinkle and shadow courageously exposed and accepted. That is how your pack will find you, that is how your mate will find you, that is how your purpose will find you, that is how peace will find you.

Journalling activity

I invite you to read the following and perhaps journal, reflect, write, meditate or create a piece of art, dance or music around the questions and your answers. Let truth flow, be honest, be open, be vulnerable and in that vulnerability find acceptance, acknowledgement and self-respect. You might even want to share your answers in our wolf community Facebook group so you can be seen, heard and witnessed by others in our pack.

So, get your pen and journal, or paintbrush and paper and let us explore...

1. How do others define you? What words do they use? What expectations do they have?
2. How does this determine how they act towards you, or with you?
3. How do you define yourself? What words or thoughts do you use to describe yourself?
4. How does this definition of yourself mould the way that you treat yourself? Do the judgements you have of

yourself affect your choices or the conditions you place on yourself?

5. What are the expectations that you feel your family or society place or placed upon you?
6. Who or what were you told you should or shouldn't be?
7. How do you want to feel about or view yourself?
8. Who are you, when there are no labels, judgements, conditions or expectations? What is left when you strip away all that you did not choose or do not want to choose anymore?
9. What does wolf symbolise or mean to you? (Past and present)
10. Why does wolf highlight is important to you?
11. Aligning with your absolute and essential truth, what actions could you take now to come into an a more authentic way of being or living?

WOLF AND DOG

The dog is the closest living relative and also descendant of the wolf and so I believe it is worth sharing just briefly some of the ways in which wolf and dog are linked in their symbolism and message and also the ways in which they differ as totem and guide. Some scientists claim that the wolf is the ancient ancestor of all dog breeds, with modern day dogs and wolves stemming from an ancient wolf ancestor.[11] So where does wolf end and dog begin?

It seems the split came about when wolves changed from fellow hunters to hunting companions, whether through necessity or divine timing. Various authorities have determined this to have occurred gradually either 10,000, 30,000 or even 50,000 years ago. The skills of humans and wolves seem to have been first used in collaboration in the hunting and then sharing of the prey, much as wolves do with other animals still. It is then assumed that this evolved to the pack defence skills of the wolf being utilised instead in defending human homes and flocks. The strong senses and presence of the wolf proved to be irreplaceably helpful in both warning of danger as a guard dog and invaluable in the hunt of other animals.

The essential difference between domestic dogs and wolves came down to being that wolves did, be and do for themselves, retaining their freedom and independence, whereas the dog was trained, or volunteered, to offer the same skills and nature in service and obedience to humans.

Dogs and wolves also both have their place as mascots, totems and companions to deities and are both present in religious iconography and mythology. However, it has sometimes been difficult for archaeologists to distinguish between wolf and dog remains that are found in ancient burial, ritual and ceremony pits. Also, when looking for evidence of the relationship between wolf, dog and human, occasionally it can be difficult to discern as to whether historic art, sculpture and references to ancient companions of a deity are depicting a dog or a wolf. They are often interchangeably referenced or depicted, hinting that perhaps our ancestors did not consider there to be such a wide gap between wolf and dog as we do now? An example of this is Goddess Nechalennia who is described and depicted as having alternatively either a wolf or a hound at her feet, with both being deemed plausible by historians and hinting at her connection to travel and fertility. The wolf or hound at her feet may have hinted at her ability to calm wild, stormy seas. There were also wolf-hounds bred for hunting, which provided a fusion of the characteristics and biology of both and were the companion of kings and male gods alike. Both these instances, however, do emphasise the companion of deity and king being hound or wolf, rather than domesticated dog, with the hunting or wild aspect of the canine deemed important enough to emphasise. Also, some wolves such as the Arabian Wolf and African wolves are, or sometimes even smaller than, dog sized, and are adapted to the hot, desert regions or conditions in which they live, giving them different features to the more well-known Grey Wolf. The Arabian wolf looks so much like a wild dog that it could very well be wolves that are the canines depicted in friezes and sculpture with the Goddesses of War, Astarte, Ishtar and Inanna.

Domesticated dog or hounds are, however, sometimes specifically mentioned in ancient mythology. An example of such is the pack of hunting dogs that rode with Welsh god Arawn through the sky that are believed by many to be the holy and divine greyhound. Also, a pack of three dogs, or a three headed dog, is often shown to be associated with Hekate, the Greek and Roman goddess, as well as Hades. In Norse mythology Hel was known to be accompanied by wolves in her underworld world, yet there was also a hound called Garm who guarded the gates of Hel. They are also depictions of Mother Goddesses with small dogs in their laps, such as Sirona and Aveta. In this context the dog, seated next to, or on, the womb of the goddess, was a symbol of the great guardianship of the goddess, as well as her fertility and abundance. Their loyal companionship and obedience to the divine also reflected the companionship and adoration dogs shared with humans.

The dog mascot of deities could also be a reminder of the connection between dogs and healing. The saliva of dogs was believed to contain healing properties and many associated divine beings were also believed to have to ability to heal or cure at will. Dogs were found at healing centres, such as at Epidaurus, the sanctuary dedicated to Asclepius, the Greek God of Medicine and at the Mavilly-Mandelot shrine and springs, dedicated to Mars. Dogs were also associated with healing gods such as Silvanus, who is often depicted wearing a wolf-skin cape, the cape being a tool with which to shapeshift, transform or change states, reflecting perhaps the transition from sick to healed. Interestingly these three healing gods and their dogs and wolves were also all linked to themes of fertility and abundance.

The constellation Canis Major was also named to depict the large hunting dog or hound that follows Orion, a huntsman in Greek mythology, as they chase a hare (constellation Lepus) or the seven sisters (constellation Pleiades). So important was this story and the role of loyal dogs, that they were given a place forever in the stars! Wolves were honoured in their own constellation of Lupus of which I share more about in Part III of this book.

The moon also has a strong connection with dogs in both symbology and mythology, perhaps more so than wolves. It is dogs that are traditionally associated with barking at the moon with many proverbs and sayings linked to this occurrence, with the dog as herald of the night, friend of the moon or calling to its mistress, the moon Goddess. Both moon and dog can represent our instincts and intuition and many believe that dogs can both travel and be present in the dreamworld. A connection is also sometimes made between their triune qualities, the three phases of the moon and the three headed dog, such as Hekate's three headed hound.

Dogs as spiritual guide and guardians and as the descendants of wolves, could be considered one branch of wolf essence or an as independent force. I have found that wolf essence sometimes considers dog essence to be pups, just like us; a younger species or manifestation. Dog does have a different essence and energy of its own to offer, with the specific qualities of loyalty, playfulness, devotion and companionship that can be emulated or used as embodiment tools and healing. There is perhaps a tamer feel to dog energy than the wild and powerful energy of the wolf, but that does not make it any lesser than, just different.

Dog energy may be different from wolf energy but sometimes it is the dog who appeals to and appears as a guide to young people almost as a preliminary step or initiatory guide if the wolf essence is just too fierce for them and their circumstances at that time. The dog or hound is often associated with the maiden Goddess's such as Artemis and Diana who are patrons of the younger self and can represent playfulness, youth and learning.

Dog is in general a gentler energy to work with than wolf and sometimes that may be more resonate or supportive for you. You might find that dog guides lead you or support you in connection to wolf energy, even as emissary, or they may work as a completely different and separate entity. The tools and practices in this book are offered for, and would work most effectively with, Wolf essence and energy but I do encourage you to further explore dog if this feels right for you. In honouring either dog or wolf, you honour the lineage of the canine genius.

Artemis Bendis Thracian goddess of the hunt identified with Artemis by the Greeks, Terracotta, ca. 350 BCE. Is she accompanied by a wolf, hound or dog? The jury is still out!

Chapter 3

Themes of healing and inspiration found in Wolf mythology, story and wisdom

In the calm, deep waters of the mind, the wolf waits.
– F.T. McKinstry

In this chapter we will explore a little deeper the reoccurring themes and symbology that are often associated with the wolf and discover what is revealed about the healing and message of wolf essence. From the lives of earthly wolves to folklore, myth and legend, these are the wolf keys and codes that are offered to you for your deeper healing and revelation. You may feel a particular resonance with one, or a few, and find you want to work deeper with a particular theme or you may just want to witness and give gratitude for the sacred purpose of wolf. Either way be open to discovering and feeling the reflection of your own journey, desires or life's themes in these different areas of wolf wisdom.

Guardians of the Threshold

Wolf can most often be found roaming the forests, the caves, the mountains and the river's edge. Wolf strolls confidently in the dark, unseen or unknown, and wild places. For most people we have only ever heard the wolf but never seen it. Wolf therefore seems to be always in the periphery of our vision and thoughts as well as literally on the edges of society, outcast and other. However, in many tales, myths and legends the wolf is in these unknown places as guide, warning or teacher. They are there so that you or the hero have a support and ally in transmuting the unknown into the known, and someone by your side as you cross the threshold where the dark turns into wisdom.

From our oldest ancestors to the present day the cave, the river's edge and the forest have been considered threshold places, the gateway between this world and the next. There has been recent evidence to suggest a stalagmite circle used by Neanderthals for ritual within a cave in France[12] and both the Ancient Greeks and Romans believed both river and cave to be entrance ways down into the underworld. The wolf is undisputed king of these places, making them its home and territory. To be at the edge, or in the dark is both their divine purpose as guardian of the threshold and as potential guide and ally in our own hero's journey when we come upon thresholds and points of initiation.

The wolf goddess Lupa acted as this threshold guide when she rescued the two twins Romulus and Remus. She took them from the river Tiber in a basket and then to her cave for their transformation from lost, threatened children to potential kings with purpose and insight. Even Red Riding Hood enters the realm of the dark forest for her own initiation and in meeting her wolf guide there she also meets her owns shadow, transmuting that fear into courage and understanding of self.

Wolves are also deeply connected to seasonal timings and can teach us about natural rhythms and cycles. The she-wolf is intimately connected with her own rhythms and that of nature and this is not displayed more so than in her retreat to her den for pregnancy in winter, to then emerge from the den with her pups in late spring. No one tells her to do this, it is not scheduled onto a phone, she is instead deeply motivated by, and honours, her instinct and nature and innately knows when it is time. The act is both practical and symbolic, reminding us that winter is a time for rest, for planting seeds in the warm earth, to offer ourselves the necessary time to be in the den, turn inwards, so that we are ready to emerge in spring with new life, vitality and clear direction. Deepen with the wisdom of cycles, death and rebirth through connecting with the she-wolf and monthly moon phases and also with the wolf and the sun's daily phases and magic. Remember that there are no endings, deadlines or full stops in nature, only transitions, shedding, gestation, growth and change.

Wolf as guardian of the threshold is your guide whenever you are transitioning from any state, time, place or stage to another. They are also a reminder of the seasons within, that reflect the seasons without. Connect to wolf when you need or want to strengthen your trust of body and soul, while deepening your relationship with your intuition. Receive the codes and wisdom of threshold from Wolf at times when the moon or the sun themselves transition, such as sunset, the dark moon or equinox.

Initiator and champion of greatness

The presence of wolf in story or folklore was often an indicator of the potentiality of those that they choose to guide and initiate. The active involvement of a wolf in both myth and legend would also often herald the presence or entry of a great leader or hero.

An example of this is again the foundation legend of ancient Rome, where Goddess Lupa comes forth to both save and initiate Romulus and Remus. Her presence marks them as the future kings and founders of Rome and it is her divine favour or interest that marks not only them but their people and city for greatness. Similarly in Lithuania an Iron Wolf appeared to the Grand Duke Gediminas in a dream as signal for the foundation and creation of a new city, which would be the base from which his nation would achieve greatness.

The Chechen peoples of Eastern Europe are also of wolf lineage and there is a legend in which their founding ancestors were raised by a wolf mother. Their nation has a saying that they are 'free and equal like wolves'.

In Italy again the Sabine people were led to new land by a she-wolf and there were offered the opportunity to create a new city where they could begin again and re-establish lineage in safety.

As can be seen, there is a repeated theme of the wolf being a catalyst for a new beginning, a fresh start and the establishing of foundations. When a real wolf establishes a new territory and pack, they will go to great lengths to find land, mark the boundaries, source the prey and create the den. It is no surprise given this expertise that they come forth to also offer their skills and knowledge in the establishment of nations, people and lineage. There example reminds you of the importance of foundations and shows you that it is essential to involve the divine, as well as sacred intention, effort and resources into creating foundations that will be long lasting and supportive long into the future.

Great heroes or significant individuals are also indicated by the involvement of wolves in their lives. For example, a pack of wolves' support and guide Goddess Leto before the birth of Apollo and Artemis, both of whom take the wolf as their mascot and companion. Our she-wolf shapeshifter and Queen, Morrigan, also acts as initiator to the Irish King Cúchulainn, facilitating tests, offering herself as sacrifice and being a catalyst for his hero's journey. The battle frenzy that was exhibited by the hero Cúchulainn was also reflected by the warriors of the wolf God Odin. Odin's name is argued by some to mean 'fury' or 'madness' indicating what seemed like possession or wolf ferocity and deadly frenzy that men exhibited in battle. This frenzy was fuelled perhaps by belief that death in battle would lead to a place in eternal and at Odin's side at the final battle. Only the greatest warriors would join Odin and his wolves in Valhalla, just as only the bravest hero could be a match for the wolf goddess Morrigan.

King Sargon of Akkad is also noted to be favoured by the War and Love Goddess, Inanna, who is also sometimes associated with the wolf. In this wolf aspect she becomes a sort of counterpart or even nemesis to her husband, the great shepherd king of flocks and agriculture. Inanna was involved in saving King Sargon, who was an illegitimate son set into the river in a basket by his priestess mother. With Inanna's favour he later goes onto to become a great king and founds a city in Inanna's honour, very much like the story of Lupa and Romulus.

The wolves teach us that we have to trust, in ourselves, our destiny and what is divinely meant for us. They ask you to consider, how can you be the hero of your own story? Their answer is to claim yourself, exactly as you are, as whole and holy. It is your authenticity that is your power and that gifts given to you at birth and strengthening through your life's experience, that signal the difference you can make and be in the world. There is a purpose for us that is as unique as we are and to be great is to be that uniqueness, unashamedly and courageously. You are the only combination of this body, sound, interests, looks, personality, astrology chart, human design, upbringing, experience, skills that will ever exist.

You are so unique, so brilliant, so mind-blowingly, wonderfully created that there is no doubt there is a path, a place and a purpose for you. Sometimes life and things make no sense when they are happening, we cannot see what lies ahead, nor a way out or up. With wolf supporting you, you will be reminded by them to trust again and again. The wolf guardians were there with those that embodied, chose or found eminence and they will support you in realising your own greatness and value.

Remember also that your greatness is not measured against any other, and how you define greatness is your own to create. Obviously, we are not all Romulus or Cúchulainn, nor meant to be, but the wolves remind you again and again that they celebrate when every single pup is born into the pack. Every pup and every wolf of the pack is supported and fed, and grows to have a contribution that only they can give.

Wolf as champion of greatness reminds you to develop and maintain firm foundations. As initiator they can support you in finding and establishing the path and purpose that is uniquely yours, so that you can grow into your greatness. Any time that you feel challenged, small, useless or insignificant, howl to the wolves and be guided by them back to the river to drink from waters of trust. Seek trust like the determined wolf on the hunt and be tenacious in your trust of the divine and divine purpose.

Howling Wolf

I expect that the image of the wolf that you are most familiar with is that of a wolf howling. It is the most commonly used way to represent wolf and this hints at one of wolfs most powerful messages.

Howling is just one of the ways in which wolves communicate with each other. It can be a form of communication while hunting but also wolves will sing together for joy. It is their way of expressing who they are and their very essence. There is something quite magical to listen to wolves when they are howling just for the fun of it!

Sometimes the howl of the wolf is perceived as something to be feared and there is often an assumption that the wolf howls in the night because it has smelt you and thinks you would make a very yummy snack. Actually, it is most often a mum or sibling wolf checking in on her kids. Think of how your mum or dad would shout down the street if you went out of the house to play without your coat on!

The wolf howl reminds us of the power of our voices. A wolf howl can be heard over many miles and so they remind us of the potential impact of our voice and words. Wolf teaches you to not be ashamed of your voice, even if your voice has been closed down or dismissed in the past. What you have to say is valuable and valid, and you can and do make a contribution. You may not truly know or acknowledge the impact of your voice, but you have made a difference to someone, somewhere and those that are meant to hear you do. Wolves also remind you to use discernment around your voice. How are you speaking and what is your true intention? Is it helpful, is it truly necessary? What do your needs, blocks and desires around speaking tell you about your woundings and areas for a deeper self-understanding and compassion?

When used as healing tool the howl can be both powerful and hugely shifting of stuck throat chakra energy but also fun and freeing. There has been just as much giggling and joy, as releasing tears and screams that have come from embodiment sessions of howling with my students!

The Howling Wolf is your reminder to use your voice for good, for liberation, for justice and for your own expression and healing. Wolves are a powerful ally for hearing and speaking your truth. Practice sounding with them, even if it means practising your expression, words, sounds or tone in the shower or alone in the woods! Confidence comes from knowing, so be the wolf pup that curiously explores, tests and plays with your voice and your body, until you know it so well you know all it nuances, needs and ways.

Wolves of the Night

Wolves are keepers of the mystery of what lies beyond or in the darkness. One association of the wolf with the darkness came from the howl of wolf sometimes heard at night time during winter months. At this time when food is scarce, wolves became hungry and their hunting may also increase leading them to hunt at dusk, dawn and darker times, as well as shorter hours of daylight. Other dark associations stem from their retreat into the cave and their connection with deities of the other and underworld.

As keepers of the darkness, they remind us that the night and the dark is not in opposition to the light, it is the other side of the same coin. Like mother and father wolf, both light and dark, day and night are both two parts of the same machine that work together for the same cause, through contributing their unique qualities and gifts. In fact, in many cultures and belief systems it is from the dark that the light comes and the dark was the beginning and the end. In Norse mythology, the end of the world will be brought about by wolf, but that very same end will be the beginning of a new world and time. There are also wolves associated with deities and myths of death, and the other or underworld, such as Goddess Hel, The Morrigan, Odin and Apollo, who all interestingly are also linked with the themes of wisdom, light, life and rebirth.

The message is that the darkness has a contribution to make, an offering and gift that can feed the parts of us that the light cannot. We therefore must roam both light and dark in our lives for balance and full integration. We contain both, life contains both, and without one we cannot achieve wholeness.

Wolves have the sharpest sight of almost all animals. They are even able to see and hunt in the darkest of nights during the dark moon. This is why we have the saying 'wolfs light' to describe the time of night when only a wolf could see what lies in the beyond and unknown.

The wolf of the night can teach you how to deepen your relationship with your instincts and intuition and to begin trusting them both. Wolf teaches you to not deny or flee from the dark but to choose instead to see in the darkness, to find the treasure that lies there. In your darkest time, call wolf to your side to sharpen your connection with your intuition so that you can follow your instinct to greater understanding and walk the path forward with greater insight.

Fear does not just go away if we close our eyes. We must face it, look into the darkness as brave as a wolf and find ourselves there. When we look at something in the day, we can judge what we see. The night takes away what we know and what we think we should know, so that we must feel instead and be led into a full sensory, heart, mind and body experience.

Wolf of the night tells you to look into the dark with open eyes, to hunt and dance with the shadows till you find wholeness of self. They ask you to be brave and look deeper, beyond what you previously considered possible. At night when all seems dark and frightening lift your wolf head up and look at the stars and witness their vastness, yet feel them close around you like an intimate and warm blanket. You never walk alone, you are supported and loved and capable.

Wolf of the Wild

The wolf is often associated with many forest beings and deities of the wild, such as Artemis, Diana and the fae; they that rule in the places where man has not sunk in their claws of control and discrimination. Wolf also accompanies the huntsman, the outcast and the lord and ladies of the forest from Red Riding Hood to Robin Hood to Pan. Like these beings Wolf is wild and untamed, there is an energy about them that is unfiltered, raw and honest. I believe the apparent freedom of 'being wild' is one of things that most attracts us to the idea of the wolf. We all long to be unfettered, and without conditions, labels and judgments.

We also long to let loose ourselves to our most innate feelings and desires, to freely explore and express all the passionate and vibrant nuances of our inner forest.

The wolf can represent or activate the wild parts of ourselves; that within us that longs to be uninhibited. As the guardians of the forest and the wildwoods they invite us there to learn our own truth and story of freedom; what for you is 'freedom from' and 'freedom to'? We are then encouraged to return to the world and our lives knowing self so deeply, that we can do nothing else but run and howl for our freedom and the freedom of the pack of humanity; to make a stand for it and reclaim it.

There is a reason why the wolf became associated with the image of the outlaw. The wolf as outlaw reminds us of the wild, untamed parts of ourselves that will not conform to societal rules or conditions. It might seem frightening to leave the path, carve out one's own way, but it is far more dangerous to lose one's own integrity and authenticity of self. It is still the most rebellious act to choose you, as you and for you.

The wolf also guides us to a deeper understand of our primal nature, so that we can enjoy it and be satisfied with life and ourselves. Wolf reminds us of the part of us that feels exhilaration when we experience true freedom, the part that longs to run naked in moonlit forests and find full body pleasure in the soft, sweet juice of a freshly picked plum. Their example is encouragement to pursue your true fulfilment. What makes your heart sing, what makes your body sing, what makes your soul sing? No one else can tell you who you are, you are your own creation! Your wildness, or those parts of you that have been called wild, are an indication of true nature, your purest self before you became filtered through societal expectations and expectations.

In the *Jungle Book*, Mowgli cries for the first time in his life when he has to leave the jungle. He has known what it is to experience being truly alive, one with nature, as nature, of nature. His tears represent the wound that is the parting from the wild side of ourselves, a wound that desperately needs healing. When you read of Mowgli's grief a part of you will recognise it as your own. That grief is a call to the forest. There in the wild you will remember that the greatest loss is disconnection from our source, our mother and nature. Following the wolf's tracks back into the forest's depths will be your homecoming.

The wolf was a commonplace beast of prey in ancient times, in many parts of the world it is only in the last one hundred to four hundred years that the wolf has been threatened in the wild and in some places extinct from that area. The retreat of the wolf runs alongside the loss of the wildwood. As agriculture became wider spread and forest land was cleared for farming and as human populations and needs have grown, so with the forests has the wolf retreated. We as the destroyer and predator have caused the loss of natural habitats and therefore the scarcity of their natural prey. What we have taken away is where wolves and their fellow forest creatures could run free and in doing so, I believe we have lost in some way our own connection to these places and the wild parts of ourselves also. It goes hand in hand. And yet, despite the destruction and threat we have caused the wolf, the essence of wolves still offers to us its companionship, healing and wisdom.

The wildwood and wolves symbolise the primitive, unadulterated parts of ourselves, an ancient part of us that in modern day life we may feel that we have also lost but remains even if hidden or withheld. It is the part if us that longs not to just see a tree, but to feel the rough edges of its bark beneath our fingers, it is the instinct that tells us to follow a certain path, that sees the leaves fall and lets our held breath release with them, it is our sense of the continuity of life and the shiver of profound awe in the presence of a wild animal.

The wild wolf teaches us that being at home with our untamed side can be empowering, it is not something to fear but to embrace. The wild wolf offers us keys to understanding ourselves and our primal nature and inspires the confidence to fully experience life with mind, body, heart and soul unbound. Connect to wolf and your wolf self by living fully in your body and including it, inviting it, honouring it in every experience. Wolf will devour the shame you have been made to feel or worn as a badge of honour. Feel wolf in the wind, with your toes in the earth, while the waterfall rushes through your hair and remember living as a sensual, fully body adventure.

Mother

Wolf as Mother is another powerful image that is shared with us in wolf legend, myth and story. There is no other animal that is as frequently noted in legend for breastfeeding human babes, signifying the essentiality of their nurturing and fiercely protective nature. The she-wolf Goddesses Lupa and Asena both rescue baby human males and then suckle and nurse them back to health and strength. These are just two occurrences where the breastfeeding She-Wolf offers herself in nourishment of mankind yet for both cultures both Lupa and Asena's breastfeeding held great significant and are remembered as profound examples of the direct involvement of the divine in human destiny.

The milk offered by these she-wolves was not just a physical transaction. From her breasts the Wolf Mother offers the milk of the goddess, the milk that represents and contains the divine knowledge and wisdom of the divine mother. Her milk is an offering of Love and the act of breastfeeding that which is lost, hungry and vulnerable is a reminder that the most powerful tools that we have are love, compassion and nurturance. Wolf as Mother reminds us that the true depth of love, the diversity of love and the power of love are the sacred tools of the mother. Love is the strongest force within you, stronger than any thoughts or ideas, pains or doubts and it is the highest frequency we can embody and manifest.

The heart, symbolised also by breasts, is at the centre of not just our physical body and the chakras, but of life and Mother Wolf reminds us of the fierceness of the heart and all it encompasses. The great courage of the mother wolf in rescuing and protecting human children teaches us to never turn away from that which seems intimidating or overwhelming; that is, the wild emotions of anger, rage, doubt, shame, fear, frustration or grief. Your feelings and emotions are part of your essential, untamed self and they are facets of love, they inform you about what is happening in your body and soul and highlight you the deepest parts of yourself that perhaps need something from you. When you feel, rage or anger, or experience intense or difficult situations, follow the example of Mother Wolf and turn towards them and ask what they are trying to communicate, what are they showing up and ask them how they want to be expressed or held.

As leader of the pack the Mother Wolf sees all and feels all, on behalf of her pack as well as herself and she leads despite the challenges that arise. She faces it head on. She feels, witnesses and acknowledges all that needs to be felt, because that is her superpower.

The she-wolf is a powerful example of the fierceness of the mother. The she-wolf represents that part of us that longs to facilitate and nourish not only our own children but all young, innocent and vulnerable. She is the mother that stands up and will fight for loving and compassionate action. Wolf seems to be a particular guardian of women and has had a deep resonance for the feminine within and without. For some, just like the orphans found by Lupa and Asena, she is the mother example that many of us did not have growing up. She offers to take her into her den and guide us as teacher and protect us as her own cubs.

Many other Mother Goddesses have the wolf as their mascot or companion, for example, Nechalennia and Goddess Isis. There is a powerful Ancient Roman image of the Goddess Isis riding a wolf that has been left to us on a relief of a votive offering. She is the vehicle to your remembrance. This image reminds us that wolf mother holds the energy of great protector that will empower all those under her care. Knowing her own strengths, she can encourage them in others also.

Mother Wolf teaches you to love fiercely and courageously. She also reminds that we have a choice about how and what we feed, both within ourselves, others and the world. What do you choose to nurture and how can you place the heart back at the centre of all you do and be?

The Wolf and the Moon

The association of the wolf and the moon appears in folklore and tradition all around the world, from Scandinavia to Native American. We also find the wolf, hound or dog sometimes as a companion of goddesses that have associations with the moon, such as Hekate, Artemis and Diana. This is primarily because of their connections to the wild, nature, magic or menstrual and women's life cycles. It is worth noting that the lunar goddesses themselves, such as Selene and Luna and Moon Gods such as the Norse God of the Moon, Máni, are not accompanied by the wolf, nor do they associate with wolves. However, we do have deities that are connected with both the sun and moon in union. Both Fenrir the Wolf and the Goddess Leto have two children, that both represent or personify the sun and the moon. In these cases, the sun and the moon are birthed from the wolf deity.

There are also solar and fire deities that are associated with the wolf, such as Apollo, Brigid, Cernunnos and sometimes Lugh.

But let us now explore some of the important connections that do exist between moon and the wolf so that we see the codes and healing that are offered to us from the union of wolf and moon.

The Wolf Moon (or old moon) in January is named so because wolves were heard howling at this time. At this time, they were on the hunt and so communicating frequently between the pack and it can be a powerful time to connect to the energy of wolf. The Wolf Moon is generally also the full moon that is closest to Imbolc and holds the codes of beginnings. It is a time and a moon that is brimming with the wolf wisdom of rebirth and of emerging as our fullest and authentic self. For many it holds the threshold before the new year and is the last full moon of the lunar cycle and so it is simultaneously both Grand Father Wolf and Wolf Pup, the beginning and the end.

The she-wolf and in particular mother wolves also remind us of the powerful relationship between the feminine, the wolf and the cycles that both move through, that reflect and are even synced with the moon. The she-wolf knows when to take herself to her den and during the winter months she surrenders to growing within herself, she takes time in the darkness before emerging in spring. This same cycle of return to the darkness to incubate and from there onwards to external momentum, only to return again and again is the same as both the moon cycle and the menstrual cycle. Is in an innately feminine process, whether for biological female animal or human. The feminine principle is the keeper of the cycles of life. A further reminder of the link between wolf and cycles is the Goddess Morrigan and the Welsh God Gwydion who are just two deities that transform or turn into a wolf as part of a series or cycle from one stage, lesson or embodiment to another.

The time of nature is different to the time of man. We are always in a hurry, wanting instant, now. Wolves and the moon teach us that everything comes in its right time, that life is not on demand with the push of a button, but that it is a process, with every stage, cycle and season valuable and necessary. She-Wolf and the moon can also teach us patience, and remind us that sometimes we just have to wait, and the waiting itself can be where the healing and the learning is present, rather than the end goal. Be in the phase you are in and know that the birthing will come, the growing will come, but do not rush the time for dreaming, holding and creating space, waiting, reflecting, this is where the foundations are laid.

Every year the she-wolf births and raises new pups, in the second and third years, her older pups teach and nurture the younger pups. She returns to the den again and again, each time wiser, older, more skilled and knowing of what is needed. Every new cycle of the moon (or menstrual cycle) is also a chance to let go of the old and brings forth something new. We grow with each new cycle just as the wolf grows its skills over time. They recognise it takes time to learn and to grow, so take each moon cycle as an opportunity.

The Wolf and the Moon guide you to release and surrender into the cycles of life, to let them be your guide to innate knowing within your body. The partnership of wolf and moon reminds you that life, death and birth all have their contribution and time.

In my courses and teachings, I guide students through the moon phases in connection to the life phases of wolf. It gives an opportunity to embody the aspects of wolf in correlation with the moon cycle, so you can connect with an aspect or lesson of wolf during its matching moon time any or every month.

This method is not dependant on whether you are biologically female but can be experienced by all. It is a potent practice and I have included the cycle in Figure 3 so that you can also experiment with this cycling. However, if you wish for a guided experience with using this format in deeper collaboration with feminine cycles also, you can do so in my book *She-Wolf*. In this book I take you step by step through the moon cycle, feminine cycles and Wolf Goddess mythology for a powerful journey of reclamation of your feminine self.

THE WOLF AND THE MOON CYCLE CHART

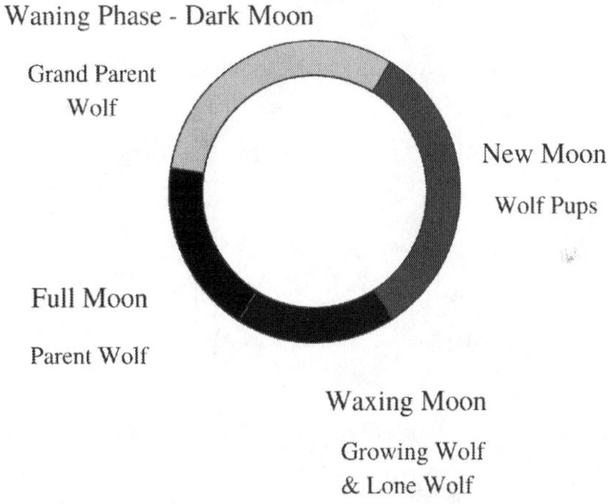

The Wolf and the moon cycle chart.

Wolves and the element of water

Wolves are comfortable with water. Both themselves and their prey need it as valuable resource and will live near or around a source of it. Wolves are also strong swimmers and have been known to travel some distance swimming in rivers and lakes and on occasion even tire their prey out by chasing them into the water and pursuing them there. There are also coastal wolves whose life and food source are primarily on the sea coast or in the sea. The water connection for earth-bound wolves is practical as a food and drink source, however, the symbology and location of the river does also arise frequently in wolf mythology and stories of wolf deities as well.

Examples of legendary Wolves that have associations with water are the Goddess Lupa and the river Tiber from which she saves Romulus and Remus, Goddess Leto's pack of coastal wolves whom save her on the island of Delos, Goddess Nechalennia, who is a coastal wolf goddess of the sea and sea travel and The Morrigan, who as wolf crossed the ford.

As discussed previously the river is a threshold place, a place which symbolises passage from one place to another and it is the Goddess, often in her wolf form as shown in the myths above, that guides, protects, steers and advises at this threshold. Those that find a wolf Goddess at the water are changed; they transform, learn, grow, cross over into a new phase or way of being.

Water is also symbolic of the feminine, flowing emotions, the subconscious mind and of cleansing. Water holds great depths of wisdom, all that is known and unknown, representing all that is moving and changing with the ebb and flow of life. Just like receiving the breastmilk of the She-Wolf, stepping into or from the water with the Wolf Goddesses also offers an ending of the old or a beginning of new life. The water symbology of wolf myth and legend remind us of the sacred role of the she-wolf as midwife and initiator at moments of change, birth, death and rebirth.

Wolves will also go to the river or a source of water while they are eating their prey to cleanse away the prey's blood from their bodies and to take refreshment. Though mostly practical, on some energetic or symbolic level it is also the offering of sacrificial blood to the cleansing and sacred waters of the feminine who gives and takes away life.

The wolf at the water's edge reminds us to connect to the element of water to wash away or cleanse anything that no longer supports our forward path. Step into the waters and flow of life with trust and nurture and establish nourishing resources both within yourself and externally where you can find fulfilment whenever you need it. Wolf also reminds you to consistently return to the holy waters to seek restoration or refreshment from the divine.

Connection to child self

Another reoccurring theme in Wolf mythology and legend is the connection with the young, in particular between she-wolves and, children or babies. In Irish Mythology we find King Cormac Mac Airt who was adopted and reared by a she-wolf with her cubs in the cave of Keash in County Sligo. Lupa of Ancient Roman legend also raised the two twins Romulus and Remus as her own pups in her cave, after rescuing them from a river and persecutors. Some stories, such as Mowgli in the Rudyard Kipling's *The Jungle Book*, also have their roots in real-life documented stories of babies or children being raised by wolves.

So why is it that wolves in particular turn up to protect the innocent and the young? Wolves are particularly known for their ferocious maternal and paternal instincts for not only their cubs, but in protection of all of those within the pack. Wolves biologically seem to have particularly nurturing instincts as well as a strong sense of belonging and identity focused around the pack.

The she-wolf in particular has three primary offerings and healings in relation to the child self; to support the healing of the mother wound, to encourage playfulness and curiosity in learning and to offer protection to those that are, or are feeling, vulnerable, lost and or young.

For those that seek to heal the mother wound, wolves can be powerful allies. They can offer the nurturing and devoted care that you may have not received from your mother. There can be a lot of pain and hurt caused in and through the relationship with our mother, grandmother or elder females from whom we have sought guidance or love. Mother wolf will adopt you and welcome you into the embrace of the strong curve of her body and support you though any healing that is needed. She offers ways to work with anger, betrayal, hurt, and grief so that you are no longer bound to the past and can come to a place of peace.

Wolf, as hinted at in its biology, mythology and legend, is also a powerful facilitator of learning. Under their great guardianship you will undoubtably be encouraged to take time for learning and growth. Have the humility of a young pup, ready to learn, when you come to your wolf guides, their wisdom is ancient and vast. When you sit at the feet of the great spirit of wolf you will receive spiritual nourishment and divine wisdom just as the Romulus and Remus did from Goddess Lupa and even Merlin from his Wolf teachers. Though the She-wolves are willing to offer their nourishment and guidance, the wolf pup also reminds you to know what to ask for! Children are also really good at asking (or loudly screaming) for what they want and so get clear on what is that you do want and practising being ok with asking. Align with your truth and share your heart's deepest howls with the wolves, or the divine, so that they can facilitate the manifestation of what is most needed and go out to hunt on your behalf.

Wolf pups remind you to consider playfulness in all learning as well. Wolves know the importance of play and pups will often play with feathers, rocks and siblings to perfect their wolf skills. Even Ivan and his grey Wolf in their story have fun along the way of their serious and sometimes difficult journey! With our pandemic of stress, it is never more important to create time for fun. Emulating or connecting to the example of wolf pup can support you in giving yourself allowance to laugh, be silly and take off any shame that inhibits your ability to enjoy yourself! Howl sing with the wolves, run with the birds, create art out in nature or remember how a stick could be a sword, a conductor's baton or a key to a portal. The child within needs play time and rest time, so honour both and don't feel shame or disgust at your body and mind's genuine needs. When our legendary children were raised by the wolf goddesses, they also learnt from them the value of rest; metal, physical, emotional, and spiritual rest. In your Wolf guides gentle care enjoy a nap or play time for the brain, heart and soul.

Wolf serves as a lesson to celebrate the innocent parts of ourselves, those parts that need and thrive from fun, learning, care and tender loving care. Approach your healing journey with curiosity and let yourself be guided with the excitement that there is always much more to learn.

The Cave

The cave has an important symbolic and physical connection with both human and animal that stretches back to the very beginning of our existence. Before man and then during the time of our Neanderthal and Homo Sapien ancestors, caves were used as shelter and home for humans, as well birthing and hibernation chambers for predatory mammals, such as wolves, bears and lions. These three predators are just some of the animals found painted upon the walls of caves and seem to have played a part in both imaginary, liminal and physical realms. Just one example is Chauvet cave, in Southern France where there are 30,000-year-old footprints of an eight-year-old boy walking side by side, seemingly in companionship, with the footprints of an adult wolf.

Wolves create their dens underground when they can, ideally with a nest at the end of a tunnel. Therefore, they often use the cave as a den space and the alpha she-wolves will retreat there for birth of pups. She will create the den in winter and the pups will emerge out late spring, around March to April, with the gestation period within the den an average of sixty-three days.

During the time of her confinement the alpha male would lead the pack for hunting and the wolves would bring food to the she-wolf. Ten days before birth she would settle fully into cave to await birth. After birth, she would be there for approximately four weeks before her cubs were ready to go outside and enjoy supervised exploration.

It is common for wolves to return to their dens again and again and there is a cave in the artic that it is known that wolves have been using for almost eight hundred years!

Like the river, the cave is symbolic of a threshold, a crossing and an entrance. Many ancient cultures, such as the Etruscans, believed that the wolf was connected to the other world or underworld as they were seen entering these caves and disappearing into the dark realms within. It is common in mythology for the cave to be the realm of the Dark Mother or the Crone, she whom we return to for death. Her realm of the underworld, was entered through caves or rivers, and primarily a stop-over or preparation time or area for rebirth into another physical life. The cave opening is therefore the doorway to the mother of death and life and the wolf who had free reign in and out of the caves and was often seen at her entrance, is a guardian of this borderland and of the threshold between her and us. The descent to her as been mapped out by thousands of years of mythology so that you have a guiding light any time when your life seemingly falls apart or you feel broken, ashamed and deeply alone. Despite the uniqueness of your own life and experiences, each stage of the process of decent and returning ascent is universal and a path long walked by Wolf guardians, so hold onto their strong, fur bodies at you take these steps side by side.

Like the mother for the baby, the wolf cave is also a place of safety and retreat for both wolf and pup. Being in the cave is also symbolic of the womb and connected to the time of pregnancy. It represents a retreat or rest before the completion of something, or a period of time when an idea, project, desire or growth develops. It was not just Lupa that took her twins into the cave to be initiated into kings, Merlin was also known to have joined the wolves within the cave of transformation for a significant time of contemplation and inspiration. Do not be surprised that when you meet and journey with the wolf essence during the rest of this book, that you also find yourself meeting or journeying with wolf within this cave of revelation and transmutation. You will also journey there for healing and enlightenment with Grand Mother Wolf in my free audio meditation on my website.

A howl from the cave calls you to journey to the deep below. With Wolf you will journey within yourself to your own cave depths, as well as those of the otherworld, to explore the womb-tomb mysteries. It is the time and space in between, it is the breath, the sacred pause. Wolf reminds you that it is from this time within that you bring forth and birth your highest and greatest potential. It is from here that can come forth deeply allied and aligned with your inner knowing.

Lone Wolf

It is very common for those within myths, legends and stories to meet wolves when they are on their own or to find the companionship of a lone wolf when they are lost or searching for something. Ivan, from Ivan, the Firebird and the Gray Wolf is such an example. Also, independent deities that either choose not to live with or have a spouse or consort are often found to instead choose the companionship of a wolf, such as the Goddesses Artemis and Skadi.

The lone wolf speaks to us about the value of time alone and nurturing our individuality. Their example reminds us that we cannot just survive, but also thrive alone and in some ways, it is actually necessary to have time alone before we return to the pack.

For lone wolves in a pack, they decide whether and when they will leave. Just like Goddess Skadi, the leaving is on their terms. Their decision is accepted by the pack and they are free to decide what is best for them, to explore and create their own pack or to return to their family. They will be welcomed back even after my years apart.

There are many, many of us that are called to wolf essence and healing because of family and societal woundings, whether they be around disconnect, disapproval, abandonment or not belonging. There is a strong connection between the outsiders of the human world and not just wolf archetype, but in particular the lone wolf. We are all searching for that place where we belong and perhaps more so striving to find that feeling of belonging and authenticity within our own selves.

It isn't always easy being a lone wolf. When the wolf leaves his or her birth pack, they are often putting themselves at risk of danger and death. They will have to hunt alone, support themselves and hold their own when they meet with other packs in other territories. We also experience feelings of vulnerability when we feel like we are the outsider, the odd one, the one that doesn't fit or hasn't found our own place or identity yet.

If the Lone Wolf stories of searching for self, ring a bell with you, then I encourage you to spend extra time with the Wolf God Fenrir's story in Chapter 7. His mythology is a strong reminder that you need not fear yourself or others, you do belong somewhere, and there is a place, and there are people, that will and can love and accept you for who you are, exactly as you are. Your worth and value is not based on whether others see it, it is intrinsic to you.

Linked in with the message of the Lone Wolf is the theme of courage. Not only is it courageous to carve your own path and to choose independence or authenticity, but wolves also courageously fight for their pack and family members if needed. Wolves have been known to even self-sacrifice in order to save family members and partners or keep their pack from danger. This is where lone wolf becomes Father or Mother Wolf, claiming the courage to know and do what is right, to fight for love and family, purpose and place, even when you have felt rejected, ostracized or wronged in the past. Lone Wolf finds strength in the wilderness and brings it back to use on behalf of the pack. They ask you: What cause do you stand up for? What is your why? What is your motivation to choose courage over fear? There will be something pure and essential to your soul intention that keeps you motivated, devoted and brave no matter what you face.

Wolves can hunt much larger animals than they are and they can spend many months alone searching for home and family, and so you can be courageous in the face of things that seem overwhelming or impossible, whether that be protecting your pups or a cause or spending time on your own and pursuing your own identity and unique expression.

Lone wolves such as Fenrir, Ivan and Skadi encourage you to search for and find yourself, for you own fulfilment, path and purpose and so that you can share your authentic self honestly and courageously. Lone wolves remind you of the value of aligning with your truth and also of purposeful time alone.

The Dangers of the Dark

A repeating theme in wolf story is that of the wolf being a creature of the dark and so therefore dangerous. Whether it be the wolf that roams the night, known only by its howl or the wolf that lies within or retreats into the darkness of the forest or cave. This retreat or hiding is often assumed to signal the danger or the evil nature of the wolf. In reality it reminds us of the dangers of being ruled by our fears as well as displaying that there is life within the darkness and it honours a creature that is confident of its own ability, and strength.

There is great potential in the dark, and I believe this is why we are led to believe it is dangerous, conditioned to fear it, to shun it within ourselves, bind and label it as evil. Yet it tempts us because of its potentiality and because of its great gifts of healing and integration. Seeds wake and grow in the dark. The dark is symbolic of death, release, rebirth, endings and beginnings. The dark is the dark of the earth to which we all return and the dark of your mother's womb from where you were birthed. In the dark lies our own potentiality, the other half that makes our wholeness and it is this that we truly fear: owning, acknowledging and being seen for ALL that we are.

The dark of the forest, the cave, the wolf den or the wolf's mighty mouth is the same dark cosmic womb from which you originated. The seemingly unknown, the void, abyss, shadowlands that are believed to be dangerous are truly full of stars, and life and the magic of creation from destruction.

Wolf is often used as metaphor for the unpleasant and unsavoury aspects of ourselves, all those things that have been labelled 'too much' or 'too little'. Yet they are a part of you, just as the wolf is part of and essential to the forest, to nature and the cycle of life. The unpleasant things that we feel and experience can also be wolf. Confusion, agony, despair, grief may seem a hungry wolf lurking in the dark edges of the forest ready to consume you, destroy you, frighten you but they are actually the very doorways to the other side. Over the threshold of being in those feelings and experiences is the otherworld, the other side where you find revelation, inspiration, wisdom, release, freedom.

What we fear about the dark is what we can't see or know . . . yet. At the same time, not everything needs explaining or understanding, and some unknown will always be that, unknown.

You are told that like wolf your anger, rage, upset and wild, untamed, emotional self is dangerous. Yet really it is your whole, true, authentic, untamed self that is most dangerous to those that which to control. It is actually your fully integrated self that is threatening to society norms, rules, limitations and conditions. A wolf is only dangerous because it is not as controllable or complying as a sheep.

The wolf does not follow or lead. Wolves work together as a pack, with valuing all and nurturing the family at the centre of everything and that is also dangerous to those that live from fear and wish to segregate and discriminate.

The wolf in mythology also tells us that both dark and light is needed. In Norse mythology it is said that the end of time will be complete when the wolves have succeeded in swallowing both the sun and the moon. And so, we will be complete when we are made whole through the assimilation of the moon (feminine) and the sun (masculine) within ourselves. A new beginning, a new way of being will begin when they are both acknowledged and honoured, within and without and work together, internally and externally in sacred communion and cocreation.

Wolf in the darkness asks you to trust the unknown, the unseen, and to trust yourself there. You may have been told, or believed that you are dangerous when you are different.

You may even have been labelled too much or wrong but wolf reminds you that is not your truth. You are not the judgements that have been placed upon you, you are a soul that cannot be contained by words or definition.

The Hunt

It is an essential fact that wolves in the wild are effective and strong predators and must hunt and kill others animals for their own food. It is probably one of the primary facets of their lives that has put the fear into humans and led to their extermination over the time we have lived together on this planet. Yet it is suspected that it was also the hunt that originally also brought human and wolf together to work in collaboration. It is also one of the only things that we still have in common, that we both kill and consume other creatures.

The metaphor of the hunt is also important in wolf legend and story. In folklore Robin Hood cleverly hunted bad guys like a wolf and in the stories of Red Riding Hood, she found herself at either the hands of a huntsman working in coalition with the wolf, or rescued from the wolf only to be hunted by man. Wolves are also the mascot or symbolic animal for many hunter and huntress deities such as Flidais and Alator.

The theme of the hunt has two important messages for us. Firstly, the hunt is symbolic of the hunt for self and it is also linked to the idea of sacrifice.

In modern life we have in so many ways become separated from our true essential nature. Yet it is possible with the guidance of wolf, to come to remember that we are made of the same earth, fire, air and water as the trees and wind. Wolf knows it is the ground upon which is hunts, it knows it is the air that it breathes and the deer that it hunts. It is therefore a part of itself that it pursues during the hunt. This hunt of the essential material that makes self is a metaphor for our own personal pursuit of self and identity, as well as the hunt for meaning in life. Every life is a hero's journey, we all have our own experiences, life lessons, traumas and strengths. Life becomes a hunt for self, belonging, love and truth. We search through different landscapes, we try different approaches, sometimes we tire and sometimes we know we are completely on the right path. Eventually we find ourselves, we meet ourselves in a wild and untamed place, and in that place that we've previously hidden, rejected or feared we catch a glimpse of truth. When the unknown becomes known then we can do nothing but be who we are and were meant to be.

The death of the wolves' prey is given to create life. The sacrifice of a deer results in the life of a pup. Wolf teaches us that from death comes life, that there is a shedding of blood, as a sacrifice in order to bring new life or renewal.

In our hunt of self and truth we will also experience spiritual blood-letting. In the hunt for self, we are required to give death to that within ourselves that is not us. As we search for own soul's truth and resonance, we must sacrifice all the ways that we have been conditioned by other and the limitations and expectations placed on us that are not aligned. This may be societal and familial bounds that suffocate us or the pressure we have placed upon ourselves in order to fit in, be right, be accepted because of fear of rejection and judgement. In finding ourselves we will have to transmute and transform in sacred alchemy the sacrificial untruths that we chose or were chosen for us.

Yet wolf does not eat to excess, only hunting and taking what they need and so we should also not sacrifice ourselves completely on the altar of martyrdom, nor allow ourselves to drown in our own sorrow, nor to bleed from our wounds to the point where there is no life left. We must use discernment and employ our inner knowing to give death to that which no longer supports our wellbeing but also to claim that which can support us, to sacrifice that which has kept us bound, limited, small and self-doubting but then give life again to confidence, courage, self-belief and truth.

The hunting wolf is well known for its stamina and can goes many days in continuous travel or movement in pursuit of prey. Robin Hood, the wild wolf outlaw was celebrated for the same tenacity in his pursuit of justice and honour. Know that like him, those that seek wholeness, to heal self and take compassionate action for the highest good of all will have wolf running along aside you, howling you on and sharing their strength.

Part II

Knowing Wolf

Chapter 4

The spiritual essence of Wolf

We are all wolves, howling to the same moon. – Atticus, Poet

In this chapter we will move on from the earth-bound wolves and their associated stories, to discover the essence or spirit of wolf. You will learn how you can spiritually connect to Wolf essence and explore pathways that Wolf offers to connect soul to the divine.

Wolves are some of the most ancient ones, from a world and reality that is much, much older than our human one. Their essence therefore offers us not only revelation and teachings beyond the now but encompasses all the wisdom available since the beginning. They offer us insight that can travel far beyond time, borders and human concepts or understanding. As this timeless essence they are sacred guardians of the ancient arts of actualisation, transmutation and soul alchemy.

Just as a new generation of pups is born every spring in wolf conservation centres around the world, so also wolf essence is rising powerfully again for a re-emergence, to offer its unique wisdom and insight in a way that can be applied to our modern needs, both personally and universally.

The Spirit or Essence of Wolf, is not the same as an animal of the same species. Living and breathing wolves are a physical manifestation of wolf energy in this earthly dimension, but wolf essence is of the spiritual dimension. When we work with totem, energy or essence of wolf we are working with the otherworld or dimensions that may or may not channel or manifest physically into this world. Here we see paradox again, of spirit and matter simultaneously, the physical wolf who roams and breathes on these lands, as symbol, representative and manifestations of wolf essence. The unique attributes of the wolf species can be manifested on a physical, archetypal, cosmic and personal scale.

In this chapter I will begin by exploring these different terms and ideas of wolf essence, energy, deity and archetype so you can gain an understanding of firstly what they mean and then secondly how they can each individually support and guide you on your path with wolf and in your personal empowerment journey.

ENERGY OR ARCHETYPE?

There are many pathways to connect with, embody and honour Wolf. The following explanations are to share some of those pathways and the ways in which wolf is present in this cosmos and reality. They are also offered to give you some guidance as to which aspect of Wolf you may want to work with. They are an attempt to put into words concepts that are sometimes beyond our human understanding or comprehension but I hope they act a tool to deeper understanding around what Wolf has to offer you, in terms of support and connection.

Let us begin with an introduction to essence, energy, archetype and deity and what these terms mean.

Wolf Essence

Essence is another term for the divine source or element of something, sometimes called the soul, the genius or spirit. It is beyond physical form and can also be considered the divine part, aspect or property of that thing that makes it fundamentally what it is. Wolf essence is ultimately the wolf aspect of divine source (divine source could also be termed as God, Goddess, Creator, Supreme Divine) just as there is also the feminine and masculine aspects. It is believed by many that that each aspect of the divine, whether it be wolf, flower, creator, chaos, masculine, feminine has a unique purpose to fulfil and offer, with its own contribution to the all and the order of being. Wolf essence is what it is to be wolf, to be wolf is to contain the essential wolf essence.

Work with wolf essence by

Taking an essence remedy or formula that contains wolf or deity essence created by yourself or a practitioner such as myself. These high vibrational formulas will support you in meeting soul to soul with Wolf. There are also many wolf allies in nature, such as plants, trees and crystals that can be taken as Essence formulas to open you to the lessons, themes and healing of wolf essence. Alternatively, you can invite Wolf essence to merge or be present with you at any time, just as you would call on or pray also to God/ Goddess. Any form of meditation or prayer and invocation would support you in connection with wolf essence.

You can also honour and visit the sacred places and times of wolf where the essence can reside, such as, forest, dusk, cave, night time, or a wolf temple. I share more about these times and places in Chapter 8 of this book.

Wolf Energy

Often energy is described as the vibration, light or the frequency of something. If wolf essence is the source of the spring, then wolf energy is the flowing water from that spring. From source it is what is transferred, channelled or manifested into the physical realms and can be felt, smelt, heard, seen or sensed. Often many people see wolf energy as blue or red in colour and you may feel or see blue or red around yourself. Wolf is also a grounding, earthy energy, which most often feels strong, powerful and direct, rather than subtle or soft. In sacred time and place you may hear energy manifest as the howl of the wolf or sense the strong pulsing vibration of being surrounded by your pack or guardian.

Work with wolf energy by

Inviting it into your meditation, ritual, song, dance or art, through openness, intention and trust. Arrive at a place of receptively through your preferred medium or practice and then let your wolf instinct guide you. You may want to visualise blue or red energy or the image, feel or characteristics of wolf in your mind's eye as you open and receive. Also notice the colours, foods and activities that you are drawn to when working with wolf energy.

You may also feel wolf energy around or within you as you work with wolf archetypes and deities. It may come through as visions, images, colours, emotions, instinct, memories or sounds.

Wolf Archetype

An archetype encompasses the characteristics and function of a particular role, for example, mother, maiden, crone or, it can be an overarching theme. There are many wolf archetypes such a Warrior Wolf, Alpha, Mother, Lone Wolf, all with their unique qualities, style and wisdom. By learning about or embodying those qualities or characteristics of that archetype you connect to a unique pathway or specific channel of wolf essence or energy. Again, if we use the same analogy as with essence and energy; essence is the original spring and source, energy is the water, archetype is a waterfall, stream, sea, rain.

Work with wolf archetype by

Considering the wolf characteristics that you most wish to embody, such a courage or aligned leadership and explore what those characteristics mean for you. Embodying an archetype encourages you to take action and emulate certain qualities or aspects in your actions, words, thoughts and intentions. For example, Warrior Wolf encompasses the qualities of direction, discernment and presence.

You can also read, then reflect and journal on stories, myths and anecdotes about wolves. Notice the tales that land with you and what they bring up, why does something resonate and what can it teach you about yourself? What inspires you and what triggers and why?

Wolf Deity

A wolf Goddess or God is a manifestation from Wolf Essence that can contain or be made of both wolf energy and archetype. Using the water and spring analogy of the previous explanations, a wolf deity would be a specific and named sea, river, type of rain, that comes from that original spring (divine source) and specifically contains water (energy). Each Wolf deity may have a particular role, offering, personality or story and may actually take the form of a wolf, have a wolf companion or mascot or instead embody a wolf archetype or characteristic. Deities are often linked with specific cultural myth, legends, symbolism and traditions, as well as representing overarching and broader themes such as wisdom, war or magic.

Work with wolf deity by:

Begin by asking for a wolf guide, guardian or deity to make themselves known to you and open up to communion. You could also research in more depth any of the wolf deities listed in Chapter 6 and create sacred time and ritual to communicate with them. Some wolf guardians may be with you for a long time, others a short time. Some may be able to help you with a specific healing aspect, such as Lupa with destiny and Odin with wisdom. A wolf deity may also be connected with a specific land, star, country, culture or blood lineage and you may want to visit the temple, land, city or holy place of that deity or their mythology.

Not included above is ancestor. The reason being is that Ancestor could be either (or all) essence, deity, archetype and/or energy. Your soul or your blood may be of wolf lineage, in that your ancestors were particularly connected with or worked with wolf and that you are continuing this tradition or re-establishing it, or that your soul lineage is connected to, or from, wolf essence. Wolf may also be connected to the lineage of the land and the energy, ancestry or deities of the place in which you were born or choose to live.

You can know that your ancestors were, or your soul is, connected to wolf without needing 'proof'. If you were to ask me 'how do I know whether I am connected to wolf?', I would say just look at the book you have currently chosen to read! I believe the fact that you are called to work with wolf is proof enough. However, it is also possible that perhaps finding this book it is a sign that it is time to begin a new lineage in collaboration and communion with wolf. Don't forget that you are both descendant and ancestor yourself, so you may in fact be the beginning.

You may want to work with a particular aspect of wolf through any of these forms of essence, energy, archetype or deity. No one way is better than any other, but each may support you in different ways at different times. It can also be useful to know which one you are working with as each may take a varied approach. Surrender and trust your knowing and intuition as to what is best for your situation and self. Remember, you do not have to have everything, logically or analytically worked out or even understand, true knowing comes from the heart, body and soul in alliance, and not just the head, so trust!

It is also true that you must *experience* to truly understand, knowledge is wasted when it sits stagnant, it only amplifies and deepens when it is transmuted into wisdom through embodiment, experience and practice. Truly honour the healing, transformative powers of union between self and wolf by feeling it, breathing it, experiencing it. This is why ritual, ceremony, and embodiment practices are so vital to growth and healing and form a vital part of my teachings. The number of times a student finds their revelation mid-dance session or during a wolf walk is testament to this!

Experience the true magic of Wolf by connecting and actively working with any of these four mediums and you will unlock your own deep inner wisdom and you will be guided toward self-realization, expression, and fulfilment.

Your experience is also not completely gender or age dependant or related. You may identify as male and still embody the archetype of she-wolf or Wolf Mother, or vice versa, you may identify as female but may find that emulating Grand Father wolf within a certain context may be most beneficial. Although earth-bound wolves may have a fixed biological gender, divine source or essence contains both masculine and feminine.

There are so many ways to experience or have encounters with any of these aspects of wolf. You may encounter wolves in the wild or at a conservation centre, you may journey or meditate with them with a particular intention or they may come to you in dreams or signs and synchronicities. Whichever resonates or whichever occurs make note of it, keep a journal and experience each as a unique thread in the tapestry of your journey with wolf. Feel free to share any of your experiences with my online community as well, there are others that your experience, thoughts and desires with resonate with as well!

In the following chapters, we will now explore wolf essence, energy, archetype and deity in more depth.

WOLF ESSENCE

Golden eyes gleam out from the darkness and we are captivated by the intelligent and noble creature, she of soft fur and sharp teeth. We are drawn in by the wolf and it speaks to something very deep within us all, that I believe goes back to very beginnings of humanity, maybe even beyond and reaches to all corners of our souls. From the depths of cosmic cave or earth forest, wolf draws us into our most hidden and ancient spaces within. We have a remembrance of wolf as kin, as collaborates in the hunt and companions in moon light runs through ancient forest. This is embedded deep into our DNA, our cells and reminds us of connectivity to source and to creation.

So, when we come to connecting to Wolf Essence, it is this remembrance, of our true self and nature, that is accessed and initiated. Working with Wolf Essence is a holy communion between souls; that source and essence of the divine and that light of essence that is resident in a human body and experience.

Why wolf?

Often, we can be drawn to a particular spirit family or essence because it contains the qualities and abilities that we as an individual need to develop or honour. If you are drawn to working with wolf essence then it has the wisdom or teachings that are most resonate for you now, or in this lifetime.

So, what does wolf stand for, contain or uniquely offer? Wolf Essence encompasses all of these qualities and it is these that we can connect to, learn or embody in our journey with wolf:

- Loyalty
- Leadership
- Community and Collaboration
- Paradox – Integration
- Honour essential self
- Nurture
- Courage
- Instinct
- Intuitive
- Playfulness

- Ferocity
- Untamed
- Fecundity
- Wild
- Liberation/ Freedom esp. from shame, fear or judgement
- Vindication
- Otherness
- Heightened Sensory Awareness including; nature connection, animal sensitivity to changes in weather, natural disasters, hormone changes etc.
- Birth, Death and Rebirth cycles and thresholds
- Tenacity
- Persistence/ Dedication
- Discernment
- Endurance

Is there a particular quality above that draws you or that you are seeking to embody or emulate? Did you feel any tingling, excitement or fear as you read them? How did your body react? What did your mind think? How did your soul feel?

Which three stand out the most for you? You may want to make note of it or circle it above on the page. You can also at this point journal or reflect on how or why you are drawn to this quality at this time. What does it mean or could it mean for you?

Wolf Essence also has these sacred and divine roles in the cosmos and creation and you may be drawn to work with wolf because you need the specific support or guidance from its area of expertise.

Guardian of the thresholds

Wolf is guardian between life and death, earth and the other world, conscious and subconscious mind. Wolf essence is a teacher of integration; roaming the caves and the forests, the edges of beyond and within, wolf calls us to look into the shadows and find wholeness, balance and harmony there. Wolf also stands with those that are stepping forward, stepping beyond, stepping up and will support you in connecting to your most discerning, courageous and devoted self.

Advocate of the Forest and the wild

Wolf is also a guide on the bridge between us and our wild, untamed aspects. Wolf highlights to us our true nature, that is, as earth beings, made of the elements, and dreamers, born of the stars. Wolf encourages within us powerful expression and celebration of the untamed and uninhibited self. With it you will nurture the authentic self and offer self the freedom to be, without shame or self-destruction.

Protector of the young, innocent and vulnerable

Wolf's mighty presence is offered on behalf of the pack, Wolf is ferocious in its protective role, guarding boundaries, creating understanding, spotlighting resources and offering safety. It will inspire within you the same fierce courage to be the warrior for the cause and together protect the young, innocent and vulnerable. With Wolf you will become the warrior that does not destroy but nurtures life, using fire and passion, strength and truth to defend, honour and protect.

Facilitator of Destiny

Wolf leads, creates and clears pathways of destiny. It stands side by side with those that choose to live a life *on purpose*. Wolf supports those that are ready to embody and actualise their divine purpose and role. Wolf is the most powerful guide to remembering, connecting to and actualising your life and soul's destiny. They will help you to figure out your unique qualities and strengths and to consider what it truly means to be you in the world and why you should do so, authentically and courageously.

I invite you now to spend a moment in gratitude and grace for Wolf and all that it is. This Divine Essence of Wolf is available to you and wanting to work with you, isn't that truly wonderful?

Wolf is a powerful essence to connect and work with! If any of these sacred purposes feel resonant to you then call on Wolf to support you in that way, to run with you as you explore the landscapes of your own truth.

When you intentionally connect with Wolf essence it will meet you soul to soul and anything that is not of spirit (limiting beliefs, emotional wounds, trauma) is brought to the conscious mind and body where it can be released or worked through in a conscious way. It is a powerful agent for emotional and spiritual healing and repair.

Wolf essence is present with you now, in your awareness and conscious – subconsciousness minds through the very act of reading these words. As we work through this book together there will be further opportunities to experience meditations and journeys with wolf essence through wolf deities, archetypes and stories. They will offer you the chance to come into presence with wolf essence and experience its profound healing and transformation. Wolf essence has and will carry you through this whole journey but now that you are aware of its particular qualities and purpose you can deepen into to receiving all that you are ready to receive.

So, now that we know what wolf essence is, represents and stands for let us next explore wolf archetypes and the ways in with wolf essence is manifest into various roles and allies that can further support and guide you.

WOLF ARCHETYPE

Working with archetypes can give you a unique pathway into accessing and healing your inner world, or aspects of self. They provide an example that can give insight into, and experience of, behaviours, habits and patterns that you currently already embody or that you wish to embody. By exploring different archetypes, you can discover what it means to become something and also highlight where you hold trauma or resistance in relation to a certain way of being or doing.

An archetype encompasses the characteristics and themes of a particular role or function, for example, mother, leader, victim, judge. I like to think of archetypes as the characters in a book, with the hero, heroine, magician, the fool, the bad guy and his sidekick all playing their part and contributing to the story. All of the characters of a story are to a lesser or greater extent, part of our personality and energetic blueprint, and at different times we can step into them, like putting on a different type of coat for different weather conditions. Often, we have judgements, conditions or memories surrounding each archetype, from when we have experienced, rejected, criticised or embraced that element of ourselves. Through archetypal work and exploration, you can connect to or channel your intuition, or your creative side, or the wise or courageous part of you. It can inspire you to explore different parts of yourself and heal the rejected, wounded or disempowered parts.

As I shared previously there are many wolf archetypes, such as Warrior Wolf, Alpha, Mother, Lone Wolf, all with their own unique qualities, style and wisdom. By embodying those qualities or characteristics of that wolf archetype you connect not only with that aspect of yourself but also to a unique pathway or specific channel of Wolf *essence.* Each archetype of Wolf has a blueprint, which is the features, the themes and the characteristics that make it up. It is useful to know the elements that make up a blueprint to help you establish what you need or desire and perhaps support an idea of what to emulate to help you reach your objective or desired end result. With wolf, most often, the end result is that you are building or rebuilding your empowered self and aligning with your truth. With the wolf archetypes you can now begin to not only consider your desires, situation, hopes, dreams or woundings and areas that need healing, but make it a reality.

The following wolf archetypes that we will explore will also offer you a chance to partner with spiritual guides, wolf essence and your highest self in order to achieve what you truly desire, whether that be peace, healing or the completion of a creative project. You will begin to unlock the what and why behind those things that light you up, that call or block you, the burning desires and the root causes of anxiety or fear.

You can also discover which wolf archetype or deity it your most powerful ally right now by taking my Wolf Archetype online quiz! In the quiz I will guide you through a series of questions that will reveal a truth about yourself and how it relates to one of the Sacred Wolf Archetypes! You can find it on my website, the link for which is at the end of the book.

Let us begin our exploration of archetype with Wolf and She-wolf. Remember that we hold both of these within us, as our sacred masculine and holy feminine, so you can embody or access both, either, all the time, sometimes. We could also see their union as the highest potentiality between our own inner masculine and feminine and also of our outer relations and collaborations. They are not an ideal or perfection to strive for with pressure and self-judgement but rather a vibrational example that is reflection provoking, as well as inspiration, opportunity and archetypal guide.

So, who are she-wolf and wolf? What do they mean? What does these two umbrella terms and overarching blueprints of Wolf essence symbolise and encompass?

Wolf

Wolf is protector and guardian. He guards his she-wolf and pups and defends his family fearlessly.

Wolf creates and holds space with his presence and consideration. He consistently walks the boundaries of the pack territory, honouring the needs and wants of the all, so that all feel respected and safe.

While the she-wolf retreats to the cave to create, channel and birth he takes supportive action, leading the pack while she travels in womb-birth time. He brings forth that which supports, provides and holds. Using his instinctual abilities and wisdom he actualises the possibilities she-wolf brings forth from the dreamtime.

He chooses to believe in the difference he can make and he knows that it is life that is at the centre and he can provide stability for it to blossom. He channels his fire into his sacred purpose and grounds it into service.

With ferocious compassion he transmutes the conditions and judgements he has placed on his personal power and with dedication and devotion transforms self-doubt into courage. Throughout this, Wolf holds the awareness that discipline should bring forth freedom, not constriction and shows up to untie his own binds of captivity.

He has full awareness of his own potential, acknowledging that with this potential comes the responsibility of choice. His mighty jaw can destroy and devour his prey, yet it is the same jaw that gently holds and moves his cubs. His power is knowing that he is both gentle, and strong, delicate and deliberate. and he takes self-responsibility for every action and word.

Wolf holds tenacious integrity and is not threatened by different or other but listens, observes, watches and takes it all in before he chooses his bark, howl or whimper.

Wolf does not need to prove himself to anyone and he knows the judgements or opinions of others do not make him what he is. He is confident in himself and learns that he is capable through the consistent practice of choosing to believe.

Wolf does not need to conquer or dominate and sees the limitations invoked by control. His power is self-sourced and do not come at anyone else's expense. Wolf utilises the strength that comes from the earth, root deep.

Wolf sees that there is no polarity, opposition is not his reality, but rather integration, wholeness, oneness. His howl rises up from root to cosmos, speaking for the pack, he is the voice that includes every member. With his sacred strength and mighty heart, he draws TOGETHER that which has been made separate, distant, opposite and opposing.

This is the way of the Wolf.

She Wolf

She Wolf is courageous. Even when she cannot find confidence, she remembers her womb deep reason to be courageous so that she does not hold back that which she must birth or create.

She Wolf hears the call to trust, and then trust again, both herself and her intuition. It is trust that will support her to navigate the process of discerning fear from truth. She Wolf embodies the traits that lead her to feeling at home and comfortable in her skin; allowance, acceptance and gratitude.

She lives in compassionate devotion to the sacredness and cycles of the land, of which she herself is made of. She remembers that both are one and the same, holy and sovereign. She listens to her body, its sighs, pains and pleasures, with the same curiosity and reverence as she listens to the wind, the bubbling brook and cry of the eagle.

She Wolf prioritizes her healing and wholeness so that she can better lead, guide and have the energy to offer her sacred medicine of empathy. She knows that only she can discern what is truly nourishing for her and so seeks and practices self-fulfilment.

She Wolf is conscious that caring for herself does mean shunning help and support from others but she strives to know herself so well that she has true clarity around what to request and what and when to receive.

She Wolf chooses and surrenders into receiving because she knows that she needs, deserves and thrives from nourishment and nurturance. She feels able to freely offer her nourishment and devotion to others when both herself and den is safe, protected and honoured. She creates pathways that guide her return to replenishing rivers.

Though it can make her feel vulnerable She Wolf allows her Wolf to provide and to listen to her dreams and actualise them. In unity, collaboration and communion they create something better together and in partnership they feed and grow the pups of harmony and balance.

She-Wolf surrenders to the flows of cycle and change, letting herself be transformed into a more authentic version of self with each experience, each turn, pivot and death. She willingly goes into the darkness of the cave, knowing the warmth there is that which nurtures growth and manifests revelation and remembrance.

She sits on the thresholds, the dawn and dusk of life, courageous queen of her domain and brings forth and manifests from a place of being able to see and feel, before, present and after.

The She-Wolf is empowered by her knowing and wise from her experience. She devotes herself to recognizing her worth so she can speak her truth and own her sexuality. She howls and whimpers her boundaries clearly and compassionately to herself and others.

She acknowledges her desire to receive the respect she deserves, so she respects herself first and teaches others to treat her, by being her own fiercest lover and ally.

This is the way of the She-Wolf.

How are you, Wolf?

Reading through the manifestos of wolf essence, what inspired you and what landed? Did anything give you a big yes and what got you curious about how it could show up in your life? If you had an "aha" moment, I invite you to journal about it now.

Let us now explore what she-wolf and wolf means for you and which aspects in particular are most relevant for you now. Not everything might call you and that is ok, we are all completely uniquely made. You are a yummy cake bowl mix of different ingredients that make and form you, and this book is about celebrating that! Your wolf guardians also know the you that the universe created, they meet you soul to soul and are here to remind you and howl you back to remembrance.

To explore the ingredients that are most powerful or relevant for you right now, I have created a chart below for you to play with!

Activity

There are a few ways to use this chart:

1. Take three different coloured pens. With the first circle all of the words that you feel you *currently* embody or feel present in your life or being. With the second pen circle around those that you *want* or *desire* to feel, embody or call into your life. With the third circle around those that

you feel *don't resonate* or feel a no towards. You may find that you circle the same word several times, that is ok! Then get curious as to the why's of all three colours.

2. You can also play a sacred game with wolf essence. Close your eyes, take three deep breaths, then open your eyes and see which three words first jump out at you. You could even do this at the new moon to channel into thematic words for your next moon cycle. This would tune you in to the characteristics or theme you will work with together with wolf essence over the cycle. You could do the same daily, once a month or during a ritual or ceremony.
3. You can use it as a form of communication between you and Wolf essence when you have something specific you need clarity or advice on. Meditate, walk, dance or breath to bring yourself into sacred space. Then ask your question or query and see which word or words you are drawn to as your answer.

You may want to photocopy the chart to use for any, or many occasions. You may alternatively want to take a picture on your electronic device to use again and again, as inspiration, or to give clarity. With it on your phone you can use it even when you are out!

Don't try to overthink it; without judgement, just go with whatever first comes to you.

If you find that the majority of your circles are in the 'both' section' this is a message to you to really choose integration, inner harmony and collaboration of your masculine and feminine.

Allow this activity to be a message from your wolf guides and wolf essence giving you permission to begin embodying and emulating wolf now. Receive their inspiration and feel their support behind you as you discern and explore what it means to step into the best and most empowered version of you!

#mywolfembodiment on social media to share your favourite words, sacred intention or message from the wolves and what they mean to you.

EMBODYING SHE WOLF AND WOLF

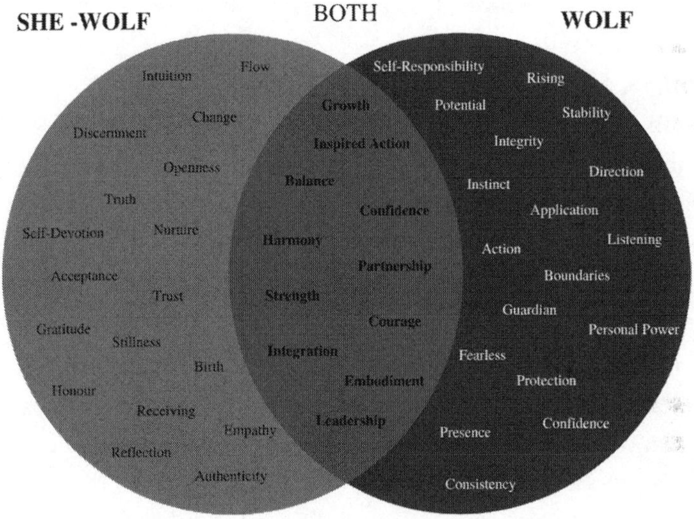

Shewolf and wolf embodiment characteristics.

THE WOLF SPIRITUAL COUNCIL

From She-Wolf and Wolf we move on to what I call the Wolf Spiritual Council, who are the archetypal figureheads of Wolf essence. Having started with the over-arching themes of she-wolf and wolf we will now focus in on seven different archetypes and their associated deities that can offer us further spiritual mentorship.

The Wolf Council are the guides and guardians of Wolf Essence. They are the council that I have been given knowledge of and worked with throughout my journey with Wolf. They are also the high council that offer mentorship and teachings in my Wolf training courses. They have asked now for this council to be shared with you, so you may know them on a deeper level, even if you have met them before in some other way or form.

They are the keepers of the wolf spiritual mysteries and codes and for some may also be soul ancestors. They also hold and guard the blueprint of each corresponding archetype and by working with them, they will reveal all of the nuances and elements of each archetype. The table below serves to highlight the unique properties or elements that each of the spiritual archetypes embodies. There are some deities given that are noted as manifestations of a specific council group but it is not exclusive to them. There are also certain wolf deities who might manifest as one archetype or another, depending on which aspect or form of themselves that are currently choosing. For example, the God Mars, is the personification of Father Wolf when he is in his Roman warrior aspect, but the personification of Grand Father Wolf when he active as the Etruscan God of farming, boundaries and vegetation.

Ultimately essence is beyond name and shape but it has chosen these relatable forms so you may have a way to understand and commune with it. Source may therefore appear to you in the form that you most need or recognise at that present time.

This table may be also helpful when you desire guidance on who to approach for support in working with a particular archetype or theme. You may want to channel or communicate with the over-arching archetype such as Grand Father Wolf or connect specifically to a deity within that archetype such as Cernunnos. Either is a pathway to the same destination.

Following on from the table is a more in-depth description of the themes and wisdom associated with each archetype to support your understanding of their role and gifts.

Activity

Working with archetypes can help you to see patterns in yourself and offer an opportunity to understand yourself deeper. They also help us to understand how these same patterns play out in others, in any relations and in society. They are universal and being ancient they offer us a connection point to the past, present and future.

As we explore the wolf council archetypes you may want to hold council with your own inner wolf. I believe your soul has chosen particular archetypes to work with in this lifetime, to learn the particular lessons it has to offer. They are linked to your purpose and learning your archetypal resonance or ally will support you in giving yourself permission to not only be yourself truthfully and authentically but empower you to utilise your unique gifts, skills and knowledge.

I invite you to take the archetypes below and write or journal about each and every one. As you do so you are invited to step fully into self-awareness and your inner archetype/s will be revealed. This activity is about tapping into your codes, without shame or conditions, so that you can give yourself the validation you crave, not seeking it from others, but recognising the rightness in the match between your soul's journey and your body, personality and lessons of this lifetimes.

This is an opportunity to reflect on your life so far and journal about the times when you embodied or most resonated with the wolf council themes and wisdom.

Take each of the seven archetypes, one at a time and for each:

1. Reflect on when and how you embodied this particular archetype. Explore why you were embodying this archetype at the time, what was the situation and how did you experience it.
2. What did you learn from this stage of your life or experience and what was the lesson or the gift from this archetype?

To take this enquiry a little deeper, ask yourself:

1. Which two resonate the most for you, or jumped out with a gut feeling and knowing attached? These two will likely be your primary guardians and embodiment archetype for this lifetime. Perhaps one, two, or three with make up your being's unique expression.
2. Were there any that you felt repelled by, or experienced a block or resistance to? There might even have been one that brought up feelings of frustration, anger or fear. This is called your shadow archetype and if you were to embody or work with it, it would reveal the route, experience or lessons that you most need to learn from to heal any wounds, trauma or triggers.

If there is an archetype that you have not experienced yet, that is ok! Perhaps that pathway is just yet to be travelled down and experienced! There is a time and a place for everything. That archetype, just like the spiritual council themselves, could in fact be one that you instead partner with in alliance, collaboration or relationship, rather than embody yourself.

Grand Mother Wolf – *She who guides and initiates*

The essence of the elder she-wolf. Grand Mother Wolf, holds the wisdom of boundaries; how, when and why to make them.

She teaches you that boundaries should always be chosen by self and that you are responsible for the flow of what and when, you receive and give.

Feminine	Masculine	Archetypal themes, elements and colours
Grand Mother Wolf *She who initiates and guides* Examples: The Morrigan, Goddess Hel, Lupa	**Grand Father Wolf** *He who listens and offers council* Examples: Cernunnos, Pan, Odin	**The Oldest/ Elder Ones** Crone, Black Sage, White Element: Ether/Spirit Wolves of the Cave, Deep Forest and Otherworld
Mother Wolf *She who empowers and nurtures* Examples: Isis, Nechalennia, Brigid	**Father Wolf** *He who protects, defends and fights for a cause.* Examples: Mars, Alator, Faustulus	**Mother/ Father** Queen, White King, Black Element: Water & Fire Wolves of the Plains, boundaries and Sea
Lone Wolf *They who lead on the path unknown* Examples: Skadi, Fenrir, Loki, Reitia		**Wanderer/ Seeker** Grey *(can also appear as mist/fog-like in appearance)* Element of Air Wolves of the Mountains and Pathways
Maiden Wolf *She who invites and seeks* Examples: Diana & Artemis	**Bachelor Wolf** *He who hunts for self and purpose* Examples: Gwydion & Apollo	**Maiden/ Youth** Brown / Red Element of Earth Wolves of the Forest and Meadow

The Wolf Spiritual Council.

She sits of the edge of realities and dimensions, before and after, guarding the threshold of cave and forest. She will initiate you in the cycles and seasons of life, returning you again and again to the deep below and deep within for full integration and assimilation.

She is loving yet fierce and speaks with true clarity and confidence that comes from having experienced the birth, life and death cycle many, many times. She is embodied wisdom and will help you to know, and then treat your body as a high temple and altar of the divine. With her your body is utilised as a portal between this realm and other. She reminds you that your body is your sacred tool of alchemy and the place of initiation; it all begins and ends there.

She never looks outside of herself for the context of who she is, she looks only inside. She enables you to remember what you do know and have always known. She says that nothing is ever forgotten or lost and that each moment, lesson, experience and breath is a key to a door.

Go to her when you need a reminder to trust and honour yourself, your instinct and to hone your intuition.

Grand Father Wolf – *He who offers council*

This is the essence of the elder wolf. Grand Father Wolf knows that wisdom is in listening more than speaking. He opens his great ears to all that is, could be and will be. He does not shout or howl to be heard and seen but rather leads by example.

He observes and watches himself and others, not from a place of self-serving, but in service to the pack. He sees beyond conditions, limitations, bias and judgements and will assist you with clarity of thought and knowing. When you let go of your ideas of what should be and listen to divine guidance, direction becomes certain.

He has let go of the need to prove himself as strong and capable and Grand Father Wolf also knows that he is a source of joy and gentleness. He will support you in trusting who you are and what you have to offer. Grand Father Wolf councils you as you release expectations and limitations created by toxic masculinity. He will guide you in fulfilling your spiritual potential and guide you in embodying patience.

Ask for his support in trusting that you are capable and he will help to open your ears fully to all the wisdom on offer; from the earth, the cosmos, the ancestors, your teachers, your highest self and wolf.

Mother Wolf – *She who empowers and nurtures*

Mother Wolf is the warmth of the hearth, the fierce embrace and the encouraging nudge that we all need when we are learning to both give nurturance to ourselves and receive it. She guides to a place of deep nourishment and self-fulfilment, and from here then teaches you how to offer and champion compassion.

Mother Wolf encourages you into self-actualisation, so that you can embrace and utilise your unique powers. She helps you to move out of the disempowerment that occurred during maiden/bachelor years and step into a leadership or queen role. Self-respect and self-responsibility are her most powerful tools of queenship. She knows that self-belief comes from self-acceptance and with her you can make decisions without shame, rather with honest recognition of your true desires and needs.

Mother Wolf, teaches you that when you are in full empowerment, you do not sacrifice who you are but serve from a place of aligned authenticity and self-awareness. Mother Wolf supports with conscious choice, as well as fierce love and tenacity.

Mother Wolf is there for those that long to live on purpose and seek to create balance between serving self and serving others. She reminds you of the value of your dreams and visions.

She will help you to nurture within you that which is truly aligned with your unique destiny, and then courageously birth it.

Father Wolf – *He who protects, defends and fights for cause*

Father Wolf brings forth his great gifts of focus and direction. He knows that he is the fire and strong grounding that gives powerful momentum and direction. He is the protector of the land and of his pack and defends both from harm and misuse.

As king of the forest, he recognises and honours his burning desire to make a difference, to make a lasting mark, a legacy. In the fulfilment of this he will teach you how to be both the fierce and brave warrior and the dependable, encouraging and affectionate father. He is a master teacher in how to use discernment and to recognise when silence and gentleness is most needed, or instead when assertiveness and speaking out would be most effective.

He reminds you that the masculine role of protector is not one you are obligated or pressured to fulfil in a rigidly defined way. It is a role that is unique as you are and can play to your individual strengths and skills. He reminds above all that his gift of safety is the sunlight that makes those under his care blossom.

Father Wolf has walked the battleground and deepest forests of the dark masculine and shadow self. He can support you when your feeling and emotional realms have been shamed, suppressed & shut down. With father wolf you will attune to your emotions and body and learn to respect them as allies. You will remember your worth and steer your passion to where you know you can make a difference.

Learn to keep your head held high as you practice being true to one's heart. Father Wolf, is he approaches life with honour and integrity.

The Wolf cubs: Maiden Wolf & Bachelor Wolf – *They who invite, seek and search for self*

The young wolves are allies in supporting the part of you that is curious and eager to learn about yourself and the world. They remind you of the value of play and the joy in discovery. Ignorance is not a vice but an opportunity and a place from which we all start many times over; it is potentiality not yet explored or considered. This archetype is for when you want to reignite within you a sense of wonder and joy. Wolf cubs are also for when you feel a pull towards times of collaboration and learning how to socialise and interact with others.

They are your guides and allies when you are also feeling insecurity about yourself, especially around who you are and where you are going. We can spend a lot of time living in and from our wounded maiden or bachelor, being the cub that is forever licking the scars from childhood. Maiden and Bachelor wolf can help you with healing these wounds and those of detachment from our bodies, mistrust and co-dependency.

Bachelor Wolf and Maiden Wolf are also extremely supportive in exploring and discovering your sexuality.

Maiden Wolf is a great ally in exploring or reacquainting yourself with your own sensuality. She also reminds you of the innocence, purity and delight to be found in all things.

Bachelor offers his humour and levity to bring lightness to a situation. When things feel like they are getting too serious or heavy he will invite you to step out of the box you have created and look to the bigger picture and expansive horizons.

The young wolves are also teachers of humility and together you can transmute embarrassment, awkwardness or shame, with a willingness to explore, ask questions, seek answers and find what most resonates or excites you.

Lone Wolf – *They who lead on the path unknown*

Lone wolf feels like a meandering, wandering spirit. They are roots that seek water, the river that flows to the sea, branches that weave through clouds. Lone wolf allies itself with those that are searching, seeking, perhaps even waiting or sat in the unknown. Lone wolves are those of you that are in a transitionary time.

The lone wolves are also those who are creating new pathways, whether that be a new career, branching away from family tradition or norms or moving on and forward from an experience. They can support your connection to your somatic inner compass and invite you into allowance.

Lone wolf eventually always finds, returns to or creates his/her pack and knows the value of the community, but also knows the importance of authenticity, resonance and of being somewhere because of true desire, rather than fear. Lone wolf knows that is important to spent time finding where you really belong, they will teach you not to compromise your essential self for approval or acceptance from those that can't honour your essentiality.

Lone wolf also knows what it is like the be the outsider; they who feels different, separate or alone. Running with them you will find that it is ok to be all of these things. Find your freedom, your wildness and revel in the ease, joy and pleasure there.

Lone wolf will help you to process feelings of abandonment and will remind you that you never lost, but always on a journey.

Hierarchy

The archetypal guardians of wolf essence do not work as a hierarchy of who is top dog, with lesser wolves below. Neither is it a hierarchy in which you find yourself ascending as you grow via age or wisdom. You can be, embody or connect to any of these archetypal guides at any time you need or desire to. The spiritual council of wolves' work as a pack and a unity, offering their own unique contribution to the whole.

They do, however, form layers of protective circles. As you will see in the *Circle of Protection* diagram, I show that the energy or essence of the wolf is circular not linear or triangular. They create embracing concentric circles of protection and guardianship.

So, just as the more experienced wolves in the physical world offer their protection to those less experienced or younger, so the whole spirit of wolf surrounds you and offers layer upon layer of strong, courageous energy upon which to seek help, support and guidance.

Circle of Protection from the Guardian Wolves.

Alliance of wolves

At the head of a real-life wolf pack is normally a partnership of a male and a female wolf, with the female wolf taking ultimate leadership and the decision making. Most wolves also form this male-female partnership, not just for mating, but for life-time companionship and form a unit of trust, communion, collaboration and co-creation. I have often found that when working with wolf essence that the same principles of partnership can be said for the deity, archetypal and spiritual manifestations of wolf as well.

These alliances often come forth when any of the following is needed within you, or in your expression in the world; balance, integration, wholeness, mother/father wound healing, relationship and partner work and healing polarity.

As an example, in my personal experience I work most frequently with the union of Lupa and Mars, and together they form an extra powerful combination for courage and destiny. They each contribute their own unique energies to create a potent harmony and balanced council. Others powerful alliances include the brother-sister combinations of Norse deities Hel and Fenrir, and Greek Artemis and Apollo. There may alternatively be an alpha pair that shows up for you that are from the wolf essence or archetypal realms, but not related to a known or named deity.

You can ask for, or may have already even experienced this alliance of masculine and feminine and if so, you are being asked to work deeply with healing the places within you that need to move from creating submission, to facilitating surrender, from fear to trust, from control to freedom.

If you find yourself working with, or even seek out an *alpha* pair, rather than just a unity of masculine and feminine then there is something within you that is been called to work with the themes and energy of leadership.

Remember the saying that behind every powerful man is an even more powerful woman? This reminds us of how the masculine and feminine work within us so that we may lead, bring forth and create. In leadership, the feminine leads from the unseen realms, the deep below and the deep within, we call forth her intuition and connection to the magic of creation and knowing. The masculine leads by actioning these dream seeds in the seen realms. The two work together in harmony and sacred collaboration. For example, if I were to create a course, the flowing ideas and inspiration would come from my inner feminine yet I would need my inner masculine to create the structure to support those ideas; that would be website set up and the sales drive. The masculine would also offer its action energy to schedule in a time and space, and make sure I show up, so that I could meditate, reflect and open up space to receive the feminine insight.

The work within to create a harmonious alliance is important regardless of gender, as we all contain both masculine and feminine energetically, emotionally and spiritually. It is important that this work be done within ourselves, before or as well as with physical genders.

There can also be present wolf archetypal partnerships that are not defined by this feminine-masculine alliance. It is possible to work with a trinity, such as Odin, Loki and Fenrir, who themselves offer the archetypal energies and themes of Grand Father Wolf, Lone Wolf and Bachelor wolf. This would be a powerful council if, for example, you wished to navigate 'what to do next and how to begin'. Loki would offer his ability to think outside of the box, as well his wit and cunning, Fenrir his bravery and independence and Odin his wisdom and foresight.

I have also known and witnessed the powerful combination of Maiden Wolf and Grand Mother wolf to bring forth firm, healthy but joy-filled boundaries. Another example is receiving guidance on truth aligned consent from Grand Mother Wolf whilst one is exploring and enjoying one's journey with sensuality and pleasure with the Maiden Wolf.

The Pack

Wolf essence and archetype, like the earthly wolf pack, works as a team. It is very likely that wolves will support you, or appear to you, as a pack. You may have several wolf allies and you will also find that your wolf guides communicate and interact with each other as well. At times when I have needed safety or reassurance, I have had a circle of wolves around me, guarding and protecting. You are one of their pack and I have found that most wolf essence actually considers us its pups. We are here to learn and they are there to guide.

I have often found when teaching or facilitating a group that we will also be surrounded by a pack of wolves, their energy and presence weaving and dancing around us. A whole family or lineage will offer their support when there is a larger group mission being created.

It is important to remember that no one wolf will 'require' or demand your 'loyalty', as all is the same divine essence and all are supporting you for the highest evolution and healing. As we have learnt already in this book, the concept of an Alpha Wolf demanding your submission through fear, control or aggression tactics is not how wolves work. They are a caring, gentle but strong energy, that will be fierce in its protection and courage but never fierce to incite fear or dominance.

Though they work and often appear as a pack, that is not to say that you may not have a particular affection or bond with a certain archetype, energy or essence. One wolf guide may be your primary guide, or stay with you for a longer period, perhaps even for life! They all have something unique to teach and show you and one may be your current vibrational or energetic match. You may also encounter singular or group human ancestors of a wolf tribe.

Sometimes lone wolf energy or deity may choose to work with you on a solely one to one basis and if this is so, know that your time together with them is for you to learn about and experience solo adventure or introverted reflection. These lone wolves are often still connected with a pack or lineage but have particular connection to the lone wolf energy or archetype and will work with you from that place. Lone wolves can also work in allyship, as well as independently just like any other wolf, it is just that their unique skills and experience lends them to teaching the wanderers, outsiders and adventurers. Don't be surprised if you find your lone wolf snuggled up back in the den with its mamma wolf occasionally!

WOLF AND THE ELEMENTS

You will also see in Figure 5 of the Wolf Spiritual Council that I have included the archetypal elements associated with each wolf archetype. However, I would also love to share with you other ways in which you can work deeper with the elements and wolf. This is something I have included in personal work, coaching and courses to powerful affect!

So, here is an overview of how wolf energy, the elements, archetypes and elemental tools can all come together in holy communion as an empowerment tool. In the following section I will take you through the five elements and their corresponding elemental wolf. The associated activities, affirmations and tools are those that you may want to include in any ritual, ceremony or energy work with that archetypal elemental wolf. All that is included is recommended for when your intention is to include the elements as a primary focus or specific healing medium. For general wolf connection tools, activities and invocations please see Chapter 8.

The elements in this format are not fixed to a member of the wolf spiritual council. For example, you may work with a Grand Father wolf that is a mountain wolf, a coastal wolf or a forest wolf. You may alternatively connect to a Fire Maiden or Lone Wolf. I have, however, included per element one wolf deity who in particular really represents and connects with that element.

Again, this is an insight shared with me by my wolf guides and guardians of which they gave permission to share with you now for deepening personal connection.

Ether Wolf.

Element: Ether – Space
Wolf Essence: Cave Wolf
Wolves of the Beyond
Energy: *I Know*
Wolf Deity Spotlight: God Odin
Area of healing/exploration focus: Connection to the divine and your divine self, trust in the universe. Also, purpose and destiny.

Affirmation: I honour my wisdom and I listen with respect and honour to both my wolf guides and my inner knowing.

Activities: Meditation, visualisation, guided journey, being in silence, dreaming, star gazing/bathing, astrological birth charting.

Elemental Tools: The circle or triangle (drawn, created or visualised) as boundary marker, an empty container such as cauldron or chalice, 'empty' space, guided meditations, colours white/grey/silver, rainbows, stillness, boundary markers, a wolf themed dream catcher, journal of dreams, thoughts and reflections.

Place: Caves, cave openings, mountain peaks, crossroads, dawn, dusk, or night time. Womb-tomb spaces of threshold or places that make you feel expansion or safely contained. Free time without intention, focus or purpose.

Air Wolf.

Element: Air

Wolf Essence: Mountain Wolf

Energy: *I speak*

Wolves of the North

Wolf Deity Spotlight: Goddess Isis

Area of healing/ exploration focus: Communication and healing blocks to communication. Bringing clarity, confidence and support with authentic expression.

Affirmation: I strive to know myself as deeply as I can, so that I can courageously align with and express my truth.

Activities: Breathwork, howls, conscious communication, writing, art and creative expression, singing, poetry, movement.

Elemental tools: Feathers (especially from the wolf allies raven/crow), incense, diary/journal or pen and paper to write your sacred words, poetry or stories on, wind, music, your voice, teeth, colours of purple and gold.

Place: Stage/ theatre, at top of mountains, hills, in a valley, upward paths, with others in community, places which create echoes, or exposed and open places.

Fire Wolf.

Element: Fire

Wolf Essence: Desert and Plains Wolf

***Energy*:** *I will*

Wolves of the South

Wolf Deity Spotlight: God Mars

Area of healing/ exploration focus: Sourcing and tending the fire (passion, focus, light) within. Finding your why. Also, willpower and direction.

Affirmation: I am courageous and I take action with purpose and sacred intent. My body is holy and sacred and I seek that which fulfils me.

Activities: Walking, running, working out, dancing, art, music, pleasure, sex, cooking, research, planning, leading.

Elemental tools: Wood, Fire/flame, Fur (sustainably and ethically sourced, or fake), candles, hot food or drinks, taste and your favourite food, oil, sexual energy and fluids, your favourite form of exercise, colours of red and black.

Place: Day time in the sun, meadows and fields, desert, near fire, with your mate.

Water Wolf.

Element: Water

Wolf Essence: Coastal Wolf

Energy: I feel

Wolves of the West

Wolf Deity Spotlight: Goddess Nechalennia

Area of healing/ exploration focus: Learning to trust oneself, honing your instincts and engaging with your emotions and feelings as sacred, valuable and insightful.

Affirmation: I trust my intuition and I am both sensitive and strong. I offer myself full honour, allowance and compassion.

Activities: Swimming, coastal walking or foraging, rain dancing, water cleansing/ blessing, drinking blessed water, washing and bathing, creating a water source for nature or ritual, such as bird bath, pond, scared pool.

Elemental Tools: Water (including fresh, salt, and rain water), shells or beach/river stones, seaweed, sand, salt lamps, bowl containing water, your favourite scent, plant essences, urine, blood, tears, colours of blue, teal and turquoise.

Place: Time near the sea, on coast, beach or in any body of water, such as lake, river or even the rain or the bath and shower.

Earth Wolf.

Element: Earth
Wolf Essence: Forest Wolf
Energy: I am
Wolves of the East
Wolf Deity Spotlight: God Pan
Area of healing/ exploration focus: Embodiment and being fully present and incarnated in your body. Respecting both your body and the earth and strengthening your connection to yourself as part of nature. Healing disconnection from self.
Affirmation: I am safe and grounded in connection with the earth and land. I belong here and I am protected.
Activities: Foraging, growing and harvesting plants, gardening, walking on the earth, forest bathing, tree meditating, taking flower essences, working with herbs, recycling, weaving, being with and caring for animals, be naked.
Elemental Tools: Soil/earth, wood, bones, herbs, herbal remedies and tea, flower and tree essences, crystals, fur (sustainably and ethnically sourced, or fake), your own hair, nail clippings, semen or menstrual blood, colours green and brown.
Place: In nature, with the trees or plants, forest or woods, garden, places where you can get your feet barefoot in the soil, create a nest or den to be in (inside or outside), with other animals.

Each of these wolves can particularly support you in their own unique way. You may want to call of the Mountain Wolves of Air when you are giving a speech or your TEDx talk, you may want to channel the Forest Wolves of Earth when you are trying to find a location to live or open to energy from the Fire Wolves when you need some motivation. I would suggest working with each group one at a time first, rather than calling them all in! You can really go deep with their specialised wisdom and healing in that way.

However, you can call on them all together as guardians and protectors of a ritual space or time, just as you may call in the elements themselves.

You as Elemental Wolf

Wolves and us are literally made up of the elements. We are a unique combination of all the elements, from our bones to our blood. We can therefore access and connect to the elements, as part of ourselves, whenever we need them. However, you will have one or two elements that are particularly strong in your personality, spirit, body and emotions. You will have been born with two primary elements as an elemental blueprint for you in this lifetime; these are elements that both make up who you are, and are important for your journey, healing and lessons and can sometimes also be reflected in your sun and moon zodiac sign.

You may also need to embody, balance or heal a certain element within yourself at any time, and the wolves can support you with this as well! Each Elemental Wolf represents an aspect and potentiality of you and offers their guidance of channelling, activating or balancing their element.

Let's consider an example. Fire Wolves, such as the God Mars, are absolutely fantastic at supporting you in finding your motivation to do something and the drive to follow that something through. Fire wolves are the wolves that are on the hunt and are all about application and passion driven action! If you are a procrastinator and struggle applying yourself, fire may be an element that is low in your personality, whereas air may be more prominent.

When it comes to knowing *what* to do, you will want to call on or channel the Ether or Earth wolves. Ether wolves will help you to connect your divine and cosmic wisdom, as well as your highest self, so that you can draw wisdom from your soul and that which is beyond you. Earth Wolves will guide you in opening up to listening to your body and your innate body wisdom. Does your body contract at the thought of something? What turns your heart on and lights up you? This is their specialism.

So, with this example, in a powerful alliance, Earth Wolf could help you check in daily with what your body truly needs or desires, such as sleep, rest, movement or pleasure, Ether Wolf can then support you in bringing sacred intent so you do so in alignment with your soul, sacred purpose or divine will and Fire Wolf would then help you to actualise it and motivate you to complete it.

In my one-to-one counselling I also have a method that reflects this, in which we consult all five elements whenever there is any decision needed to be made, or clarity desired. Derived from this method I have created the following activity. This discovery session is for you to discover your intrinsic element and which elemental wolf matches your elemental birth blueprint. Perhaps you already felt a familiarity while reading the profiles above, but I hope this will provide you with some further insight into your own being and offer an opening for deeper work with your wolf guides.

Elemental Wolf Activity

Have a read through of these descriptions and choose the one that best describes you. There is likely to be a second one that also has some familiar or resonant parts. Make a note somewhere or tick the first and second below, that feels most like you. With no judgement or condemnation, I invite you to be truly honest, only you really know you and who you are behind and beyond all of the expectations, limitations and conditions placed upon you. Answer for who you are, not who you think you should be.

Elemental Wolf 1

My life lessons and my journey have often been themed around transferring my imagination, thoughts and ideas into reality and finding ways to express and communicate them, and myself. I am always learning to find a balance between stillness and movement, neither too much or too little. My key is grounding in the swirling and finding the stillness when I'm inclined to rush. My biggest challenges are procrastination and indecisiveness.

I am most content when I am out and about and am happiest when in open spaces and not confined. The horizon makes me feel free and exhilarated. I enjoy movement but have to remind myself to find also take the time to fully breathe out as well as breathe deeply in.

I seek out solitude to reflect, read or write, and I love to share my thoughts and ideas with others through writing, drawing, speaking or singing. I often need time alone to charge and day dream. I am the wolf that will travel to and from the den, journeying onward and outward, then returning to ground, and repeat. Others may consider me a bit flighty, sometimes only hearing from me occasionally as my mind is busy navigating my inner and outer worlds.

I am the wolf who gnaws on the bones. I am happy to peck at food and I love the socialising and talking that happens at meal times, just as much, or more than the food because of all that I hear, smell and see. I therefore like to eat with others and discuss the day or what we are eating.

I am the wolf that howls. I have lots of thoughts swirling around, sometimes I can struggle to put the concepts or thoughts in my head into words. Finding ways to bring my imagination into reality and sharing it will others is something I experience daily. I do like to reflect on and consider my words before I communicate.

Elemental Wolf 2

My life lessons and my journey have often been themed around establishing boundaries that support and hold me rather than block or limit me. My emotions can also sometimes feel like an overwhelming flood or a mist in which I get lost and I am learning how not to be overwhelmed by all that I feel. My key is to surrender and trust and see that what is soft can also be powerful. I am learning how to learn to ride the waves and take in the view, rather than exhausting myself in fighting the current.

I feel most content when I am near water, whether it be the seaside, near a waterfall or a long soak in the bath. I am the wolf that likes one paw often dipped in the cleansing, clearing waters whose bubbling and flow caresses my soul.

I am the wolf that feels the hurts, sorrows and joys of my whole pack. I relate to others through their emotional bodies and have great empathy for others. What I do, when I do it and how I do it, is determined by how I feel. I am happy with others or alone, and can flow easily from company to time alone.

I am the wolf that easily goes with the flow when it comes to dinner time! I sometimes eat a lot, sometimes little and work best without strict meal times, so I can eat what I feel like, when I feel like it. I particularly like my food to refresh me, it is the well I go to when I need healing and I follow my instinct as to what would best serve my well-being nutritionally. For me it is important to know why I am eating and not to eat mindlessly.

I am the wolf of growling. What I say is often a reflection of my emotions and emotional state. I can speak for long periods of time, sometimes it is hard to stop! There are times when my words and emotions just bubble up and my speech can be quick and fast. Expression naturally flows through me and I find my clarity through expressing my thoughts and feelings. Getting the words or sounds out can even support me in releasing and cleansing.

Elemental Wolf 3

My life experiences have taught me about honouring my needs and attuning to the wisdom and joy of my body. I love to give but one of the biggest lessons I am learning is also how to receive. I can get really comfy where I am and even when I know the need to find a new den, or go out and hunt I find myself hesitant to move and prefer staying where I am. My key is to nurture me first, so that I can then be my best and fulfilled self, and in turn share my gift of nurture. I am learning that I ground to rise up, not to stay stuck and that my deep roots are to support my growth upward and forward.

I am the wolf that roams the forest and you will often find me sat at the base of a tree or off the beaten path. My paws will be deep in the earth, whether it is speaking to, growing or dancing with plants. I love to collect flowers, pinecones and sticks to take back to my den and when I can't be outside, I bring the beauty of nature inside through my creations.

I am often the mamma or papa wolf at the centre of any pack. I relate to others easily and they feel safe around me. I love to see people ripen and I try my best to be compassionate to all. My pack is very large and pups are naturally drawn to me to be nurtured. I can be a grounding influence.

I am the wolf that always gets its fill and I often graze eat as food is enjoyable and pleasurable to me. Food also helps me to ground and it reminds me of the needs and desires of my body. I am good at responding when I am hungry, which is quite often! I show my love to my family by creating food for them and enjoy providing an abundance of nourishing food for the pack.

I am the wolf of whimpers. I have a natural way of knowing the words that will nurture and support others. My communication is generally warm, honest and gentle and I am really good at listening. Often, I am told that I just know the right thing to say when needed. I also use my body to communicate, using gestures and touch, physical communication for me is just as much important as words.

Elemental Wolf 4

Finding my purpose, making my contribution and how I serve the divine are the most important aspects of my life. I have a deep awareness of myself as part of the cosmos and find great peace in regular communion with the divine and my guides. I have sometimes struggled with disconnection or separation from this reality, and I have felt frequently like I don't belong or don't quite fit. I am learning to incarnate fully and be in this human experience and body, to embody all I know, to ground my wisdom and share it. My key is remembering that I chose to be human for a reason, that this body not only serves and supports me but is an anchor and safe harbour for this journey and my soul.

If I can go within then I am content. I like to spend time reflecting and I value the peace and quiet to do so, away from the pack. I therefore have a place or space that I go to regularly that is just my own. I prefer quiet spaces but also love to be in nature, or places where I can acquire knowledge, learning and greater understanding. You will find me in sacred, holy spaces, created or established that speak to my soul.

I favour time on my own. I am not always a lone wolf but sometimes I can find it difficult being with others because I can trigger or baffle them. Conversation with me is always deep! I do best as a space holder and like to watch and observe others. I am reliable, value integrity and I am always there when people most need me in times of trouble or crisis.

I am the wolf that is last to the buffet, I tend to eat when I remember. Creating, making or enjoying food isn't very often on my mind or it isn't a priority. When I do eat it is intentional and I love to form ritual or ceremony around it, even if it just starting with a blessing before I eat. A community created meal suits me or one that consciously come from communion with nature. I remember that food is a gift from the divine and how and what I eat can be affected by my energy levels.

I am the wolf of silence. I love to listen to others, hear many perspectives, hold space for others to speak and then reflect on what has been said. I like to share my voice but only when I feel it is truly necessary and when it is sourced from my deepest wisdom. I am the wolf that speaks for the all, with all-encompassing consideration.

Elemental Wolf 5

I am wolf that has learnt and is learning how to wield the sword of discernment. I have wounds of being called 'too much' yet I have a growing awareness of my power and my ability to create and destroy. I sometimes struggle to shine my light, fearing that I will burn others, scare them away or that the light will be stolen. I like to be active and doing something, sometimes anything, just so that I don't have to sit idle or waste my time. My key is to remember that it is not always either, or. I can be gentle and powerful, loving and strong, ferocious and compassionate. My warrior spirit and powerful personality is an inspiration, but also holds responsibility, I am learning to be patient and channel my passion wisely.

I love to bask in the warmth and have the sun or heat upon my fur. I need places I can explore, wander, run and walk. I am curious about all the places and things not yet done and I am happiest when I can stride up a mountain or discover a new path. You might even find me rolling around, playing in the grass.

I find pleasure in being in the role of leader or teacher, and I find that sometimes this can happen even in my closest relations. I like to guide and inspire but sometimes get impatient with others when they don't keep up. I am the hunting wolf and I am lit up by searching for that which will feed myself and my pack, physically, emotionally and spiritually! Patience and standing still is something I need to learn in order to support how I interact with my pack.

I am the wolf leading the hunt and I love to create the food I eat. I find researching ideas and recipes enjoyable and searching for and buying ingredients fun. I am quite open to most foods and will try new things. My meals are either a masterpiece, really tasty or something I've spend some time and energy considering or planning. Eating is a pleasure and can be a passion. Often it is even a sensual act.

I am the wolf that barks. I tend to talk quite passionately about the subjects that I love, but I am easily bored and loose interest with that which doesn't inspire me. I can be firm, sometimes stubborn in my ideas and viewpoints. My voice and communication can be powerful, sometimes even getting quickly heated! I have to really concentrate on listening because my mind is already racing ahead!

1. If elemental wolf 1 spoke to then you are an Air Wolf.
2. Or you may feel that you are most like number 2, the Water Wolf.
3. If 3 resonated throughout your body, then you are Earth Wolf.
4. Or you felt a deep connection to number 4, then you are Ether Wolf.
5. If 5 lit you up, you are match for Fire Wolf.

Make a note now of your top two; your primary element, and your secondary.

As you read through the elemental profiles you may have found that certain parts of you related to different elements.

For example, you may think like an air wolf, eat like an earth wolf (both your inner self) but act like a fire wolf (your external self). If this was the case for you, you may want to call on the air wolves when you need to come up with a plan, the earth wolves if you want to begin a healthy eating regime and learn how to channel your passion and to achieve your goals with the fire wolves!

Also, I should note that if you are in any way a spiritual person, to a certain extent Wolf of Ether will be an aspect or an essential part of your being. I imagine most of you will find it in your top three!

But whichever had your biggest YES, that highlights to you your elemental blueprint and your elemental wolf archetype. Your secondary yes is your supporting element.

You may want to journal more as to why that element spoke to you, what insights it gave you into your essence and you can paint, draw, write or dance this element and wolf as an extra activity. Perhaps again you want to share this with me or our wolf community!

Now that you know your primary elements, you can work with your elemental pack by exploring and enjoying further the recommended tools, activities and affirmations suggested under each wolf and dive deeper in the element with the support and guidance of the wolves. This does not exclude from the other elements at all! You can embody, try out or step into any element when it best serves or supports you, and the wolves of that element are only too eager to help.

In the last chapter of this book, I have included an invocation to your elemental wolf that you may want to speak, pray or write in your journal now to bring a conclusion or moment of gratitude at the end of this chapter before we move on. You can also use it any time you wish to work with the elemental wolves to commune with them, to honour them, or to open space.

Most of all let this elemental attunement and revelation be a celebration of the characteristics that make up you. Sometimes, such as in this activity, you can see yourself reflected in nature and the mystical, and it can offer you a validation of who you are, and offer permission to be you, utterly and completely! No part of you is essentially wrong, even when there may be parts that need healing or growth.

From seeing your personal magic highlighted by your elemental wolves, feel a greater confidence that you are uniquely made, and made with purpose. You are a combination of strengths, experiences, offering and skills that no one else has. You were made this way so that you could contribute you, not an imitation of anyone else. So don't dim your fire, hold your breath, stay buried in your roots, or dam back your emotions. *Every* wolf is needed in the pack, and there would be a large gap if you aren't authentically filling it. Take a deep breath, affirm your sense of belonging as of, on and with the earth and deeply connected not only with your earthly, but also cosmic purpose.

I invite you to set up some sacred space and time now before we finish to acknowledge all that you have felt, realised, remembered and learnt in this whole chapter.

We have in this chapter deepened our connection to wolf essence, energy and archetype. All that you have learn, felt and explored so far will carry you forward as you deepen and strengthen your reciprocal relationship between you and wolf essence (divine source). Learning about and then connecting to the archetypes, spiritual council and elemental wolves is all part of this beautiful reciprocity, which opens a window for conversation to start happening! Instructions, and guidance will be come through, so listen, trust and be curious.

Know that your wolf guides will also continue to with you as we now move forward and explore the final of the four aspects of wolf; Deity.

Having journeyed through the ethereal lands of wolf essence, in the next chapter we are going to now explore a little deeper Wolf as deity and symbol in God and Goddess mythology and legend.

Let us witness how the essence, archetypes and energy of wolf has contributed to and manifested in our human lives as deity, God and Goddess. It is not intended to be an in-depth analytical look at history but rather a celebration and revelation of the profound and powerful presence of wolf essence in spirituality and an exploration as to how you can incorporate wolf deities into your spiritual practice and empowerment journey.

Chapter 5

Wolf and the Divine

The wolf has been associated with many deities, gods, goddesses and divine beings. Often deities are associated with wolves because the wolf symbolises a characteristic or attribute associated with that deities' persona, such as strength, guardianship, or cunning. Other times the wolf is connected to a deity because of a role that the deity and animal both perform, such as healer, leader or mother. Sometimes divine beings can also morph into wolves or use them as messengers. Others actually are a wolf, living and being manifest in that physical form, rather than being temporary shape-shifters. There are also references to wolf figures working on a divine or cosmic level, though not in direct association with a particular named deity, such as the ravening wolf of Germanic mythology whose consumption of all life, in heaven and earth, leads to the rebirth of the universe. We also have historical and archaeological evidence for priests of wolf cults and deities, the most famous being in service to the deities Lupa and Apollo. And the saying "a wolf in sheep's clothing" may have also originated in priests, priestesses or shamans having the ability to shapeshift into animal form, or channel and receive an animal spirit such a wolf within their human body.

The wolf meant different things to different belief systems, cultures and traditions. This is reflected sometimes in which deities are associated with wolves or which attributes of the wolf are most celebrated by being deified. For the ancient Romans the deified she-wolf was both founding mother and guardian of Rome as well as a term for prostitutes, reflecting both the varying, sometimes polar viewpoints on both wolves and women. For the Norse the wolf was symbolic of chaos and inevitable destruction, as personified by the God Fenrir. Yet Odin's wolves were also one symbol of his great wisdom and guardianship. This may reflect both the fear and the respect that the Norse felt for the abilities of a top-ranking predator.

Whether the wolf symbolised life or death, or both, is an interesting reflection on the culture who held that viewpoint. It reflects not only their spiritual beliefs, but their fears, hopes, values and discriminations. It can even give us a window into the everyday thoughts and feelings of ordinary people, what was worthy of note, what did they worry about the most? What was so important or feared that they deified it or saw it personified in their deities?

As we will discover in this chapter, just as the symbol and idea of Wolf can mean both shadow and light, so Wolf is also connected to a diversity of deities that has associations from birth, abundance, fertility, children and motherhood, to, death, war, hunting and the underworld. Whatever the viewpoint, the repeated association of wolf with the divine does undoubtably affirm that there was a belief in the magical or mystical abilities of the wolf. There is no doubt that our ancestors had a great respect and even awe for the wolf and its abilities and skills.

Let us now dive into some of the associations, mythology and symbology that connects the wolf with divine and otherworldly beings. We will explore the wolf deities of the past but as the divine transcends timelines and spaces, remember that they are also still present for us now, with gifts, messages and healing that we will see is still relevant and potent. They may have belonged to our ancestors but we can also reclaim and choose them for ourselves. So read what is shared as both a witness and as an open-hearted explorer who seeks what is most resonant and needed right now for self and humanity. Follow the initiation maps that are found in the mythology and legend of wolf deity that can give you much-needed context and guidance through your own peaks and valleys of embodied life.

Wolf Goddesses

Let us begin with exploring the wolf and the goddess. The she-wolf has associations with almost all aspects of the Goddess; maiden, lover, mother and crone. It seems to be an all-inclusive symbol, the she-wolf able to embody various roles spirituality just as she does in the earth-bound pack.

Firstly, let us explore Maiden and Wolf. Maiden in the context of the Goddess often refers to the status of being unmarried or un-associated with a male consort or counterpart (just as virgin means whole and holy unto one's self), rather than being a reference to sexual immaturity or lack of sexual activity. We mostly find the wolf associated with not just the maiden goddesses but more specifically the huntress maidens. In their mythos we find them to be fiercely independent, take lovers on their own terms and create a life that is about exploration and self-fulfilment. Within the context of the Wolf Spiritual Council, you will find that these huntress Goddesses mostly embody the archetype of the maiden and, or, lone wolf.

The wolf is a symbol and companion for both the Greek Artemis and Roman Diana, as well other maiden-huntresses such as Celtic Goddess Flidais and the independent Lithuanian Goddess Medeina, who was said to favour the company of pack of wolves to any man. The wolf for these specific goddesses symbolises their independence, the prowess at the hunt and their guardianship of the wild and untamed physical places, as well as guardianship of beings that are yet untamed and unfiltered by society and life. Wolves then, as companions of these maiden goddesses, can also be powerful allies to those such as young children, teenagers and adolescents. They also champion the inner child of us all, the young, innocent and wild aspects within ourselves that may feel vulnerable, undecided or as yet unexpressed in the big, dark forest of life. The wolf and maiden goddess team ultimately serve as a reminder of the freedom we must claim for ourselves so that we can grow into ourselves and to teach us how to be tenacious on our hunt for discovering who we are and who we can be.

Another wolf goddess who embodies this independent huntress spirit is Goddess Skadi. In her mythology and Norse tradition Skadi is the Goddess of wilderness and winter. In her story Skadi finds herself in a marriage with a God not of her choosing. They both have very different desires when it comes to where and how they will live. Skadi chooses to part ways with her husband rather than sacrifice that which she knows brings her true joy and peace; the snowy mountains and the wild peaks. She bridges the place between maiden and lover and is a powerful ally for those that seek to self-source their own pleasure and fulfilment. Her mythology reflects the time period of the lone wolf and she is often depicted with a lone wolf companion to personify this. Sometimes she does also appear with her pack of wolves as a reminder that even as a lone wolf our heart is meant to love and be loved. Our pack is important but it is just as important that *we choose* one that matches our highest values, principles and authentic self. Her mythology sets you an example to pursue a life that is truly aligned with personal desires and dreams rather than being limited by the expectations, demands or conditions of others. She is the lone wolf that bravely honours her heart and soul and tenaciously seeks her own self-fulfilment.

Wolf has also often the companion of The Mother Goddess or Mother Goddesses. Hilda Ellis Davidson in her *Gods and Myths of Northern Europe* shares that the symbol of a large canine is often also depicted alongside Mother Goddesses, particularly in the Roman Period in Celtic areas, as her most consistent companion and mascot. As already explored the dog, hound and the wolf, were particularly associated with the Mother Goddesses because of corresponding themes of great guardianship and protection. The she-wolf in a pack, like The Mother Goddess, is also the ferocious leader and the matriarch that guides, nurtures, feeds and gives life.

The Capitoline Wolf, as known as Lupa, stands guardian of Romulus and Remus, just as she does over the city of Rome.

A great example of the Mother Goddess as she wolf is Goddess Lupa. In her mythology Lupa rescues the twin babies and future founders of Rome from the river, before taking them to the safety of her cave to be fed and nurtured. As the mother of the Romans, she become a symbol of an Empire that was also both fertile and abundant, and her breastmilk was the symbolic nourishment that provided life and vitality so that Rome and all Romans could thrive. Lupa is also the Mother of the Wolf lineage in Europe, she is also the Etruscan Grand Mother Wolf, the energetic blueprint, womb and origin of the biological *'C. arnensis's line which gave rise, via the Etruscan Wolf, to the Grey Wolf, which was to become the most widespread wild mammal in the world, spanning Europe and Asia and crossing to America 700,000 years ago.'*[13]

Also associated with the Mother Goddess, are the wolves in the Greek story of Goddess Leto. She is led by wolves to a water source on the island of Delos, in order to drink and so she can survive during her banishment. This Goddess of fertility and motherhood is not only supported by the wolves of Delos in finding sustenance during her exile but also significantly the wolves were said to be with her during her prolonged and difficult labour. With the support of the wolf pack, Leto goes on to successfully birth Apollo and Artemis, the sun and moon. Leto is a powerful Goddess of labour and birth for this reason and can support you with any fears, trauma or worries around birthing your own pups. Goddess Diana is also a well-known Wolf Goddess who shares the similar aspect of wolf companion, associations with childbirth and as a guardian to labouring mothers.

We also find depictions of the wolf with the mother goddess in her queenship aspect. One such Queen deity is the Great Mother Goddess, Isis. There is a fascinating Graeco-Roman votive patera depicting Isis and a Wolf with human twins beneath her.[14] The picture seems to be a meeting of Egypt (Isis) and the She-Wolf of the Roman Empire (Lupa). It is not clear as to whether the intention of the depiction was that Isis is using the She-Wolf (Rome) as her mount or whether Isis was being equated with Lupa. Both are Mothers that share primary importance in the foundation and creation of a great nation. Both, through their divine intervention, spiritual midwifing and breastfeeding of kings, founded and influenced two of the most significant cultures in European and North African history. They represent the wolf as sovereign queen or alpha of her pack as well as the mother as nurturing leader and the point of potential destruction and creation.

Goddess Lupa is often depicted suckling her foster children and defending her young. Even without the children beneath her she is almost always shown with breasts full of milk. One of the most popular images of Isis is also her breastfeeding her son, the divine child, Horus, while supporting him with her other hand. Given all we have learn about wolves so far it is not surprising that the wolf chooses to accompany the Mother Goddess, reminding us of their shared divine role as protectors, guardians and the milk-wisdom source to kings and nations. The ferocity of the mother wolf to defend her pack and pups must have been well known by ancient peoples, or the Goddess chose this mascot on purpose for their shared strong maternal instincts to defend and nurture. Both Lupa and Isis are significant allies for anyone that is wanting to create, to manifest or bring forth that which is unknown into the known, to make ripe that which was unripe and to grow aligned with personal destiny and sacred purpose.

The she-wolf as guardian is also associated with the outcast and is known to have been the Goddess Protector of those that have been ostracised by society. Italian Wolf Goddess, Reitia, is the Goddess charged with protection of the foreigner, as well as travellers and those that are lost. She is depicted as wolf, with her wolf form is this context symbolising human fears and otherness. She is the goddess guide for those that are outplaced, that perhaps feel they don't belong or are searching for that belonging. We are reminded by her of the lone wolf that leaves the pack and roams, looking for her or his place to create a new pack. She also reminds us of the dynamics of a wolf pack and the importance of working together in unity to create a collective identity where all are accepted for their unique contribution and all are valuable, including the weak, lost, old or different.

Goddess Hel, Wolf Goddess of Norse mythology, also represents those that are outcast or shunned and her wolf symbology reminds us of the lone wolf that makes her own way when separate from the pack. She is a wolf goddess because Hel's siblings are wolves but also there are said to be wolves that guard and roam her underworld or otherworld as her companions, often sitting by her throne. Like wolf, she is an ally for those that feel different to everyone else or that are considered the outsider. In her mythology, recorded in the Poetic Edda and various Norse poems, she is sometimes appointed, sometimes forced into being the ruler of the underworld. Being considered frightening and dangerous, in part due to her lineage but also her looks, the underworld is the place deemed best to place her, out of the way but still doing something for the gods. Hel is, however, fierce and courageous and does her job well. She offers an eternal home to those that die from old age and illness. She displays a sovereignty in taking ownership of her fate and what others may consider a bad lot, she turns into a purpose and divine role. She acts with the cleverness and insight of wolf, carving her own role independent of her father and the other gods. Her authority and position are also not dependant on a husband or consort. As Goddess of the underworld Hel also embodies the archetype of energy of the Elder, Grand Mother Wolf, she who sees and knows death and can guide through any transition or transformation.

Welsh mythology also has its own She-wolf by the name of Rhymhi or Rhymi, whose two wolf cubs are sought by the hero Culhwch. She, however, proves to be both fast and clever and it was noted that she defended her pups with devotional ferocity. She, like other she-wolves, was considered dangerous, firstly because of the wild shape and form she used in the protection of her children, but also in her independence. She is an outsider, made deadly by carving her own way and life, with no obedience or loyalty to a ruler. In her story, however, she is eventually returned to her human form, back to a human queen, and her sons are taken from her. Her independence, freedom, right and ability to defend her cubs is quashed by the hunting men. Part of her importance is her role in providing an initiation or quest for Culhwch by encountering the Goddess in Wolf form. This is an initiation that only the Goddess can offer, where she takes on the role of sovereign queen that initiates the seeker into the attributes of the knight or king; bravery, determination and wisdom. Her story also offered a moral tale about necessity of order, through the taking of the cubs away from the wild, untamed feminine to the orderly and disciplined court of King Arthur. The She-Wolf Rhymi bridges both the archetype of lone wolf and mother wolf, by embodying both.

The she-wolf in mythology, just like the Goddess, represents both the potential of life and death. She gives life in the form of Lupa or Isis through her breastmilk, through defending her children like Rhymhi or defending outsiders like Reitia and as Leto and Nechalennia through the gift of sacred waters. She also stands at the doorway of the womb-tomb, with the Crone Goddesses of the otherworld and transition, such as Hel and The Morrigan and also with Diana, a Goddess of childbirth, at the crossroads where the maiden dies and becomes Mother. Many wild and untamed beasts become associated with death as well as life because death can be perceived as a ravenous beast, with no exceptions to its unquenchable thirst. So, we find that the wolf, as the predator that hunts and kills its prey, is often associated with goddesses of death and the underworld. And so, the paradox of light and dark simultaneously that wolf so well represents, is yet again displayed through its Goddess associations and its diverse affiliations with deity.

The she-wolf as Goddess ultimately highlights the important role of the wolf as guardian of the thresholds between this world and the otherworld, between before and after, as well as protector of the various transitional states and initiations that we will all undergo throughout life. The den of the she-wolf can be seen as the womb of the Goddess, a symbolic place of death, birth, transition and transformation. In many cultures and traditions caves were seen as openings to the underworld or inner world and as the same time it was seen and known that she-wolves in particular would use the cave as both home and den. The She-wolf specifically would disappear into the darkness for unknown time, entering her den, only to emerge with pups many months later. This time within and below, whether for birth or travelling to Hel, makes the Wolf Goddesses potent allies for journeying to your great within, whether the within be represented by the womb, forest, cave, or places of exile and wildness. The mythology and symbology of she-wolf and goddess are important for teaching us about the necessity for aligning with our truth and trusting our inner knowing so that we can then take purposeful direction of energy, thought, and action. We create great ripples with every paw that we place on the earth and in the water, so for the example of Goddess as Wolf and discerningly conceive with intention and incubate dream seeds in the great below, before courageously navigating the resulting changes brought forth from those seeds.

In summary, the wolf goddesses are here to support you with

- Connecting to your wild maiden; cultivating independence and self-fulfilment.
- Integrating the parts of you that you have exiled or deemed bad, wrong or ugly.
- Healing the mother wound and support you in learning how to be a vessel of creation and nurturance.

- Journeying to the otherworld or underworld to align with truth and bring forth new life.
- Guiding you through times of threshold or change and initiating you into your highest self so you can live on purpose.

Wolf Gods

As well as the Goddess, the wolf has also been frequently associated with the gods. One of the most well-known wolf-god alliances is with the Roman war god Mars. Mars, was originally a god of vegetation, agriculture and a guardian of boundaries and fields, with many of his festivals linked to farming season markers. He protected the farms, crops and livestock presumably from wolves, as well as other threats such as birds. However, as the threat became human rather than animal and those land boundaries became more often crossed, fields more frequently fought over, Mars assumed a major role as God of war. He became a protector of the men that worked the fields, as well as the fields themselves and then the men that went to battle and war in order to attain more land. However, both Celts and Romans regarded Mars has having a role like the Alpha wolf, as peaceful protector, healer and tribal God. He represented Father Wolf who protects and guards his pack, hunts for food and leads bravely and wisely. In this role as hunter, protector and leader he was often assimilated with other male deities across the empire such as Mars Lenumius and Mars Loucetius as well as being associated with Celtic gods such as Cocidius and Braciaca, some of whom has links to wolf in their iconography or myth. Mars's temple in Rome contained many images of wolves and the wolf was known as one of his sacred creatures, along with the woodpecker.

The image of the wolf came to represent Mars as military mascot. The wolf was in this context a symbol of ferocity and strength or power. Along with boars, ravens and even geese the wolf came to have an association with battle, as an inspirational example for the warriors to embody. All four of these animals also have associations with guardianship and protection.

Mars's wolves were shown as devourers and dangerous, deadly fighters and his warriors in battle were encouraged to emulate this, as the main objective in any war was to win. His wolves are most often depicted as black, the same colour that the Norse god Fenrir is often described to be, in reflection perhaps of their deadliness and the fear they inspired or as this colour was associated with death in these cultures.

Fenrir, the wolf God has been labelled with the same ruthless and deadly ferocity as Mars's wolves but he himself was not just associated with wolves, but actually takes the form and body of wolf. Son of Loki, Fenrir was shunned by the other Norse Gods and was captured and bound by them as Odin was told that he will be consumed by Fenrir at the end of time, Ragnarök. It was also due to his lineage that Fenrir was expected to be aggressive, troublesome and deceptive, with it being said that only the God Týr having the courage to feed him. Týr later loses a hand in the mighty mouth of Fenrir when Fenrir was deceived into an unbreakable fetter. I share more of Fenrir's story, healing and wisdom in Chapter 7. I feel him to embody the archetype and energy of bachelor Wolf because of his great prowess in supporting you in discovering the truth of you are and shunning and giving death to the expectations and judgements of other.

In many recounting Fenrir serves the purpose of representing the chaos or destruction that is always ultimately inevitable. He also serves as a vehicle through which the bravery of another God (Týr) can be demonstrated, with wolf being deemed the most ferocious adversary due to their strength and fearlessness. These writings reflect the perhaps negative associations that the wolf had in Norse culture and Fenrir was feared, just as the wolf was, rather than being worshipped. Another occurrence of wolf in Norse Mythology was the turning of another of Loki's sons, Vali, into a wolf, who then immediately attacked and killed his brother Narvi, in which the Norse belief in the wolf's deadly and dangerous nature is re-emphasized.

Loki's brood; Hel, Fenrir and Jörmungandr. by artist Emil Doepler (1855–1922).

Fenrir's nemesis Odin, God of battle, as well as wisdom, poetry and the sky, also has an association with wolves. Along with his ravens, his wolves were said to both feast on the slain in battle and to be present in Valhalla.

> *The raven together with the wolf, is mentioned in practically all the descriptions of a battle in Old English Poetry, and both were regarded as the creatures of the war God, Odin.*[15]

Their attendance was a signifier of the presence of the war God, the apparition serving as both reminder and warning of the death that comes to us all. Even Odin himself would one day be devoured by the Wolf. The stark reminder of our eventual demise by these allies of Odin served to encourage his followers to die well; that is, with honour, with courage and for a cause. Just as the wolf will ferociously fight to defend its pack and its family, so Odin's warriors were called upon to show the same valour and to be driven by divine purpose, not personal gain. Odin's two personal wolves that sit by his side at the throne of Asgard, also remind us of his affiliation to the Grand Father Wolf archetype. He is the wise wolf that sees all and thinks before it acts, with an all-encompassing gaze.

The wise wolf or Grand Father Wolf archetype is also with associated with Celtic God Cernunnos, 'the Horned One'. He is the God famously depicted on the Gundestrup cauldron and shown seated and antlered surrounded by wild beasts, most predominately stags and a large wolf. As the Lord of Nature and the animals, Cernunnos may have also had associations with fertility and abundance and is considered to be one of the oldest depictions of a Celtic God. He is considered to be anthropomorphic, appearing as any of his associated wild beasts, just as often manifesting as the stag as the antlered Man-God. So, when he appears to you, he may also in fact appear as a wolf, rather than with a wolf. The Romans associated Cernunnos with their God, Mercury, who was both messenger and guide of the dead to the underworld, both of which are also wolf themes and roles. His solar wheel also reminds us of his ability to change and transform, as well as of cycles and seasons. The wolf and the sun both hold the energy of fire, creationship and powerful action, as well as also the potential of destruction and consumption. Both sun and wolf can destroy or grow that which is under it and so Cernunnos as Grand Father wolf symbolises wise guardianship and the discernment to choose who to be and how to be.

This connection to the sun is important for wolf gods, such as Cernunnos and the God of light, Apollo. There are also other wolf gods that are linked to the element of fire, such as Mars and the Norse God, Loki, father of Fenrir the Great Wolf. Fire, the sun and the wolf, all remind us of their potentiality for life and death. The sun is also a symbol of power, both personal and regal and can illuminate, both literally and metaphorically. Fire is the element of direction, of action, passion and creation. In ancient Egypt the God Upuaut, whose name means opener of the ways, is often depicted as a white or grey wolf standing at the prow of a solar-boat. In this one image he encompasses all that the solar wolves stands for. The sun and fire wolf gods see all and stride forward as the creators of pathways. He is movement and action, the forward momentum towards actualisation and revelation.

The Greek God of Light, Apollo is an interesting Wolf God, that simultaneously embodies Grand Father Wolf, Father Wolf and Bachelor Wolf. An interesting story that reminds us of his energy as God of Healing and Disease, is linked with his manifestation as Soranus Apollo. In a mountain temple dedicated to Apollo there were Hirpi (Hirpus meaning wolves in Faliscan) priests that would perform rites and sacrifices to the god. On one occasion wolves ran off with the intended sacrifice and took it to a cave. On entering the cave in pursuit of the wolves, the men chasing were all killed by poisonous air. This was followed by the local communities becoming afflicted by a deadly disease. When an oracle of Apollo was consulted, he saw the wolves as an important message from the god and told the priests that to appease Apollo they must *become like wolves*, meaning that like the cave wolf they must undertake the role, rituals and rites of gatekeepers of the underworld. When this was done Apollo would lift the disease and no one else would die. This story is a reminder of the wolf's guardianship of threshold between this world and the next and the belief in the wolf's ability to use the caves as a portal to the underworld or otherworld. As wolf that guards the entrance to the underworld and death, Apollo embodies the archetype and energy of Grand Father Wolf, he who sees and hears all.

Apollo's association with wolves, however, began long before his birth as his mother Leto was assisted by wolves, who helped her in her banishment and difficult labour of him and his sister Artemis. They were regarded as the sun, Apollo and the moon, Artemis. Some legends say that his mascot wolves were chosen in honour and remembrance of their preservation of his mother Leto's life by guiding her to water. As the rising and new son or sun, Apollo embodies the energy and archetype of Bachelor Wolf. It is in this embodiment, and as God of music and song, that he can support us to heal our howl and express our heart's melody.

As God of light, music and disease, Apollo was a God of joy and sorrow, life as well as death. He was responsible for centres of healing, as well as being responsible for plagues and pandemics. Apollo is, therefore, also another example of the wolf of paradox; light and dark, death and life.

Charun, sometimes called Calu, is a wolf also associated with death, as well as the underworld and afterlife., He was an Etruscan wolf God, fearsome ruler of the underworld, sometimes described like Fenrir as the 'monster' with the head of a black wolf, flaming eyes and large fangs and has a large hammer to crush skulls. He was a terrifying figure to the Etruscans, in the form of the wolf who is associated with death, through the wolf being predator and its ability to kill. The Latin for wolf 'Lupus' possibly derives from the earlier Etruscan word 'Lupu' which means 'to die', with the word Lupus referring to "the dead".

Charun is an interesting reflection of the fears of the people and culture within which he is based. I share in my book, *Lupa,* that, just as wolf can still personify fear for some people, Charun arose:

> *in Etruscan tomb and funerary art in the mid-300's BC at the time when Etruscan culture was itself in its last death throes, and the fear of destruction by Rome was deeply ingrained into the minds and hearts of the last Etruscan peoples. At this time, it seems that the afterlife was viewed as a terrifying place, just as life may have also seemed.*[16]

We could then see the wolf gods are an interesting reflection of the perspective on death within a particular belief system. For the Etruscans the afterlife was unpleasant and they were a culture that celebrated living, death being a far cry from the vibrant and richness of life that sought to create. The wolf, as Charun, therefore becomes a deadly, devouring figure for this life loving, farming and trading culture. In was in some ways a Lone Wolf, who personified feelings of being lost, abandoned, uncertain. In contrast to this, the afterlife of Valhalla of the Norse was a place where the brave and worthy who has died in battle would be honoured, celebrated and thoroughly enjoy themselves. Here Odin's wolves sit by his side in Valhalla, a symbol of his cleverness and the wisdom of the wolf. Their place in the afterlife was a reminder of the courageous ferocity of wolf and reflected the braveness of the warriors, for whom death was a reward, not something to fear. Likewise, to die well was important for the Romans and the Father wolf became a mascot for God of War, Mars whose warriors would die the best death, that is in honour and sacrifice for the empire, for the emperor and for the expansion, abundance and continuity of Rome. Death for the Celts was to journey to the otherworld, where the gods resided. It was the land of wisdom, knowledge, from where the gods and ancestors offered not only their protection but also insight, revelation and inspiration. As a reflection of this we find Celtic gods such as Cernunnos and Alator as Grand Father wolves of wisdom and guardianship.

In summary, the wolf gods are here to support you with

- Connecting to your inner warrior; cultivating integrity and courage.
- Give death to your fears of not being enough and failing. As well as reclaiming the parts of you that have been shamed, judged and criticised by self.
- Diving deep into the roots of your power and healing any wounds around choice, control and failure, so you can trust your sovereign self.
- Learn to listen to your primal body as guide so that you can attune on the deepest level to your truth and potentiality.
- Guiding you through the underworld to access your own inner wisdom and find the heart centre of what you fight and live for.

Chapter 6

Meet the Wolf Gods and Goddesses

In this chapter I will share the principal healing, messages and wisdom of each of the wolf gods and goddesses. This is the manifesto of each wolf deity discussed in previous chapters as well as some other deities that I have not otherwise explored in detail but deserve their place here in this sacred roll call of wolf essence. All of these deities have some connection to wolf, whether it be as symbol, mythology, mascot or archetypal relation. Some are depicted with a wolf as companion or mascot, some change into a wolf and some actually are wolves. Each has their own unique connection to the energy, themes and archetypes of wolf essence and so every deity is accompanied by a brief explanation as to their connection with wolf essence as well how they can support you in your life. I have also included their associated archetype in relation to the Wolf Spirit Council, as well as their primary and secondary elements. I have also listed their sacred Wolf colours which may be the colour they appear in (or with) their Wolf mythology and tradition and affirmed through my own experience and the testimonials of my students and clients. This includes the colour of the fur, energy, and, or, aura and may be different to or the same as the colours sometimes associated with their symbology or other manifestations.

You may want to include these deities in your work with wolves, or you may find that they appear during visions or meditations. They may have already appeared and you want some help in identifying who it is that came to you.

You may alternatively want to use this guide to find out which wolf god or goddess could be your most potent ally right now. In someone stands out to you take it as a sign to work deeper with this energy! It might even clarify what it is that you are seeking.

WOLF GODDESSES

...a she-wolf coming down out of the surrounding hills to slake her thirst, turned her steps towards the cry of the infants, and with her teats gave them suck so gently, that the keeper of the royal flock found her licking them with her tongue.

The She-Wolf, Goddess Lupa, finds the twin babies at the river's edge, beginning their initiation to become to founders of Rome. Story told in the ancient Roman text History of Rome Vol 1 by Livy

Lupa

Archetype: Grand Mother and Mother Wolf
Element/s: All the elements but in particular Ether, Water and Earth
Colours: Gold, Blue, White and Grey

Lupa is the She-Wolf of Rome and Mother of Destiny. She is a Roman and Etruscan deity who is the energetic mother, blueprint and essence of all the wolves of Europe. The earth-bound European grey wolf also claims her as its biological source and ancestor. Just as she initiated Romulus and Remus, Lupa is a most powerful guide in helping you to remember, and then live, your purpose. She is the mid-wife and wet nurse to kings and an empire and she reminds you of your own unique destiny and facilitates the awakening of the tools and wisdom within you that can actualise that destiny. She will support you as you step into your power and seek the highest and truest expression of self.

She will often meet you at river's edge or in within the cave. Call on her as teacher.

The Morrigan

Archetype: Grand Mother Wolf
Element/s: Fire and Air
Colours: Black, White and Red

The Morrigan is an Irish goddess of life and death, magic, shapeshifting, and war. She is also an initiator in the cycles of life, but in particular offers her guidance and wisdom when you are traversing challenging or difficult journeys or moments in time. She is a guide and guardian when we find ourselves in the dark and unknown places of self and life. She will show you the necessity of death as a portal of birth. She will support you as you work with fears and worries, helping you to take them through the three stages of transmutation; destruction, preservation and creation.

She will often appear as you are going through the threshold of transition and change but you can also call on her when you are ready for change as well.

Skadi

Archetype: Lone Wolf
Element/s: Air
Colours: White and Grey

Norse Goddess of the Mountains & Winter and Queen of the Ice. Skadi's lessons are those of independence and honouring self. She will invite you to step out of comparison to others, to trust yourself and to keep to your own track with conviction and devotion. She is a lone wolf but creates and chooses this for herself, knowing it as a necessary path for her own fulfilment. She will help you navigate the seemingly endless mountain terrain of possibility.

Connect to her as the snow wolf, meet or work with her in the mountains or during winter. Look for paw prints in the snow.

Hel

Archetype: Grand Mother Wolf and Lone Wolf
Element/s: Earth and Ether
Colours: Black, Blue and Grey

Norse Goddess of the Dead and Guardian of the Underworld. She is part of the Wolf family with her father Loki and her brother the wolf Fenrir. She provides a home to all those that die of sickness or old age, a land of mist and shadows called Niflheim. Her wolves assist the souls of the dead over the threshold. She teaches about sovereignty and being queen of the path and purpose that is given to us. Her lesson is: do not live in resentment of those things you cannot control but claim what you are given as yours to do well. She is the noble, determined and cunning energy of wolf.

Work with or call on her at dusk or dawn or through mirrors and your own reflection.

Brigid/ Brigantia

Archetype: Mother Wolf
Element/s: Fire
Colours: Red and Gold

Brigantia or Brigid, Goddess of the Tribes of Celtic Britain and Queen of the North. She is sovereign queen and represents the power and potentiality of the feminine. She will support you in embodying Alpha She-Wolf and leading with grace, compassion and self-awareness. Or connect to her as Brigit or Bride the Celtic goddess of spring, fertility, and life. She is the Mother Wolf of Fire that supports growth and creation. She is a powerful guide for birthing and midwifing anything new that you which to start or manifest, such as ideas, projects, relationships.

Ask her to protect you and what you are bringing forth like her own pup. With her call on the wolves of the north.

Reitia

Archetype: Lone Wolf
Element/s: Earth and Air
Colours: The grey-brown of earth paths and roads

Italian Wolf Goddess of Foreigners and outcasts. She is ally and guardian to the exiled, the outcast, the refugee, the nameless and socially excluded. She heals the reasons for and the ways in which choose division and segregation. Like the wolf that is made wrong, and bad, she asks us to reflect on the parts of us that we fear and so fear to see in others. She is also a wolf that will support a group or community of people.

Call of her any time that justice needs to be done or honoured. She is also a powerful guardian wolf when you are travelling or making a journey, keep her talisman in the car or rucksack.

Artemis

Archetype: Maiden Wolf
Element/s: Earth
Colours: Brown or Grey

Greek Goddess of the Moon, chastity, the forest, the hunt. An ally that will support you in the archetype of huntress and aligning with your true, free and uninhibited self. With Artemis you are encouraged to take your bow and arrow and aim at the heart's truth of what it is you truly desire and need. Her lesson is one of discernment and stamina in the hunt for self-discovery. She is a powerful maiden wolf that will teach you independence and what it truly means to have freedom.

Artemis favours working one to one. Find her, in quiet, while in the woods or forest.

Diana

Archetype: Maiden Wolf
Element/s: Earth
Colours: Blue, Gold and Silver

Roman Goddess of wild creatures and places, protector of children and childbirth. Diana can support you with the reclamation and healing of your maiden self and will then guide you over the threshold into mother archetype. She can support you in birthing your truest self as you integrate all parts of you that have been previously limited, victimised or condemned during childhood or young womanhood. She will also support women during the birth of children. Ask her to protect and guard the she-wolf den that you choose for labour.

She loves to work with you in correlation with the blood mysteries and your menstrual cycle. Connect to her, and howl, at time of the crescent moon.

Isis

Archetype: Mother Wolf
Element/s: Air
Colours: Red and Gold

Egyptian Goddess of Motherhood, healing and magic. Isis is connected to wolves through the Mother Archetype and also through her teachings of spell work and spoken magic. She is a potent guide in supporting you with the reclaiming and power of your voice and speech as tools of creation. Together wolf and Isis can offer alchemical healing, activation and empowerment of the throat chakra. She is the Mother Wolf that helps you to express your wisdom with clarity.

Connect to Mother Isis when you need to utilise the power of words or want to heal any aspects or woundings around motherhood or queenship.

Elen of the Ways

Archetype: Mother and Lone Wolf
Element/s: Earth and Fire
Colours: Brown

An ancient Welsh and Roman Queen who was married to the Wolf King, Macsen (Latin Maxen). Like the boundary marking wolf she created pathways so that a way home to Wales could always be found. She will support you in affirming your sense of belonging and identity. A wolf always knows and remembers for a lifetime the smell of its pack and family pathways. She is the guardian of Hiraeth and teaches you to confidently follow the signposts that your soul offers.

Connect with her when you want the wolves of protection to guard your home or space. Also, call on her for trust and intuition when travelling or making a journey.

Rhymi

Archetype: Mother Wolf
Element/s: Earth and Fire
Colours: Red and White

Rhymi or Rhymhi is the Welsh Mother Wolf who ferociously guards her children and finds herself set against the knights of King Arthur's Court fighting for independence. She is the she-wolf that rebels against all the ways in which the feminine is told she should always be *just* good, gentle, soft and emotional or is deemed lesser than because of these traits. She is She-Wolf that stands for the value of women and the opportunities to determine their own identity, path and choices. She is a particular ally for anyone that feels they are being confined or judged by the expectations that are placed on the feminine. She will give you strength and courage.

Howl with her for your rights and your sovereignty. Call on her when you need to be firm.

Flidais

Archetype: Maiden and Mother Wolf
Element/s: Earth
Colours: Brown

Celtic Goddess of Wild Places and things and Divine Huntress, believed to be of Irish origin. She is associated with wolves, as their guardian and protector. In Irish mythology she is often depicted as a Queen of the woods. We may ask Flidais for her help and support in re-establishing and guarding the great forests of the world and reintroducing wolves into the wild in a sustainable way. When witnessing the life cycles of woodland flora and fauna she can also help us to understand deeply and intimately how all those in nature serve and support one another.

Call on her support when you meet real life wolves or walk in the forest, woods, or nature. Ask her to bless and protect both.

Cynthia

Archetype: Mother Wolf
Element/s: Earth and Fire
Colours: Red, Gold and Blue

Celtic Goddess of the wild and Queen of the forest. She will support you in creation of sacred space and time that is in alignment with the truest and highest benefit of mother nature. She will encourage you to trust nature and trust yourself as nature's ally and co-creator. She is the Mother wolf that creates the den for the future and lays solid foundations. She will help you find sustainable ways of living and being that are in alliance with the earth.

Connect with her when you are seeking resources to create, build or birth. She will come to you at times when a den of any kind is needed or in production.

Leto

Archetype: Mother Wolf
Element/s: Water and Fire
Colours: Blue, Red and White

Greek Titan and Mother Goddess of the Moon (Artemis) and Sun (Apollo). She is the strength and determination of mother wolf.

After assault by Zeus, she was exiled to an uninhabited island, to birth her children alone, shamed and terrorised by Hera. The wolves came to her as support and led her to nourishing water that ensured her survival. She was also accompanied in labour by a she-wolf/wolves. She will support with self-resourcing and reclaiming your value and self-worth. She will show you what it means to truly love yourself when all seems lost and hopeless. She is the Mother-lover wolf who offers her care to women and children and heals wounds around abandonment or betrayal.

She offers her wisdom and support to those that seek to heal the wounds of a past relationship or work with a partner to align with values and the divine. She also will come to you when you need integration of the she-wolf and wolf within.

Nechalennia

Archetype: Mother Wolf
Element/s: Water
Colours: Blue and White

Germanic Mother Goddess of Sea, Travel and Fertility. Often shown depicted with a coastal wolf, Nechalennia is a guide for those that are navigating life and trying to find their way. If you feel lost at sea, in emotions, worry, or uncertainty she is your guide! She is a powerful ally for those that are on a journey, whether physical or metaphorical. She is the wolf that longs to find its way back to a place that is open and trusting of source. She will help you trust your instincts. She is the mother wolf that offers a compass to find your way home to the den no matter where you are.

Connect to her at the coast or near the sea. She may come to you when you are working on creating true abundance in life.

Circe

Archetype: Lone Wolf and Mother Wolf
Element/s: Earth, Water and Fire
Colours: Black and Gold

Circe is Titan, Queen of Beasts, Sorceress, Enchantress and Witch of Aeaea. She is also a Greek Goddess that holds the powers of transformation and protection. As daughter of the sun and the sea, she is a powerful ally for balancing and harmonising the paradox within and of processing the alchemical uniting of shadow and light. Wolves were one of her companions in her exile, she was said to tame them through her very nature. Circe is a powerful ally for those that wish to connect deeply to nature as a healing tool and access their inner abilities, or magic, to transform and transmute.

Call on Circe as a witness and space holder to your invocations, affirmations, rituals and ceremony. She will support you in using all the wolf lessons as tools of creation and transformation.

WOLF GODS

Lycaon fled, terrified, until he reached the safety of the silent countryside. There he uttered howling noises, and his attempts to speak were all in vain. His clothes changed into bristling hairs, his arms to legs, and he became a wolf. His own savage nature showed in his rabid jaws, and he now directed against the flocks his innate lust for killing – The Punishment of Lycaon in Metamorphoses by Ovid

Mars

Archetype: Grand Father Wolf and Father Wolf
Element/s: Fire
Colours: Black and Red

Mars is the Roman God of War as well as courage and guardianship. He is also the earlier Etruscan God of boundaries, spring, fertility and agriculture.

The black wolf is Mars's sacred animal. His wolves are the wolf that uses strategy, ferocity and strength during the Hunt and War. His power is in service to the pack, for defence as well as nurturance through providing food and protection. Mars symbolises, and gifts to his followers, warrior energy. He is the Alpha wolf that fights nobly and honourably for a cause, he that leads with a brave and fearless heart and defends the young and vulnerable. He is both Father and Grand Father Wolf and he reminds you that the sword has the power to wound or liberate, you it wisely and purposefully.

Call on Mars during times when you need Courage or want to access your personal power.

Pan

Archetype: Grand Father Wolf
Element/s: Earth
Colours: Brown

Pan is the wild, primal and untamed Lord of the Woods. He is the arcadian God of nature, the wild, mountains, shepherds, flocks and wild animals, who is often associated with sexuality and fertility. He will guide you in coming into your body and fully experiencing its wisdom and signals. He will open your ears to the subtle and powerful wisdom of your physical self, deepening your connection to yourself as made of the earth. With him you will experience a heightening of the senses and intuition.

Pan is your ally for embodiment and somatic therapy. He will support you in releasing negativity or shame of your wild self or body. Meet him in the wild parts of nature, dance with the trees and in the river.

Fenrir, also called Fenris

Archetype: Bachelor Wolf, Lone Wolf
Element/s: Fire
Colours: Burning Black, Brown and Red

Fenrir is the Great Wolf God and part of the Norse wolf family, as son of Loki and brother of Hel. In his myth he is deemed deadly and as a result is treated badly through torture and fetters. He is punished for being dangerous but continues to break free of his chains. He is representative of the wounded masculine. He is a powerful guide for breaking free of the bonds, expectations or limitations placed on men around being masculine. He challenges us to ask and address our judgements and conditions around what the masculine should be, and what it should do, feel and look like. He will help you to release yourself from the confines that make man, or being man, solely violent, wrong, bad – and give death to these labels so that man can step into his true energy, fully integrated and embodied.

Fenrir comes to those that are ready for liberation and release. It will devour your negative judgements of self. You may want to meet at the threshold of dusk or at night.

Faustulus

Archetype: Father Wolf
Element/s: Earth
Colours: Brown

In Roman mythology, Faustulus was the shepherd who raised the children Romulus and his twin brother Remus after they left the care of the she-wolf Lupa. From him they learnt the way of the shepherd. He can teach you how to be in the role of guardian and how to compassionately and courageously provide guidance and leadership. He teaches how it essential for any king to embody empathy and compassion. He is a great guide for those who wish to trust and be trustworthy, though you may be suspicious or condemning of the wolf within and without. He will support you in seeing what is most just and how truly powerful kindness is. He is a powerful ally for creating feelings of, or structures that cultivate, safety.

Call on Faustulus especially when you need the patience of a wolf and the trust of the shepherd. Meditate with him on the plains or in the crop fields.

Gwydion

Archetype: Bachelor Wolf
Element/s: Air and Fire
Colours: Silver and Red

Welsh Magician and God of Magic and Trickery. Gwydion was cursed to turn into a wolf as part of his punishment for the crime of rape and so experienced the life, body, needs and hungers of Wolf. Gwydion is a guide in understanding and healing polarity to gain a deeper comprehension of the world and life. He will show you that it does not need to be all or nothing, or always a choice between extremes. Balance is not too opposing forces, but the place where they meet in equality and harmony. He tells you that true knowing and the most potent magic comes from the integration of your shadow and light. Ask him to help you with balance, especially if you feel yourself overwhelmed or consumed by emotions, energies or conflicts. He is bachelor wolf who is learning what it means to find wholeness.

Gwydion is the guide for those that find themselves embodying the angry, rapacious or rabid wolf and wants to transform this into harmony, peace, generosity and patience.

Lycaon

Archetype: Father Wolf
Element/s: Air
Colours: Grey

Legendary King of Arcadia who tried to trick the Greek God Zeus into eating human flesh. In order to determine whether Zeus was indeed the greatest of the Gods and all-knowing, Lycaon had his son killed and served as a dish in order to see if Zeus would notice. Zeus did notice, of course, and transformed Lycaon into a wolf as punishment. Lycaon's arrogance and cunning was seen as similar to a wolf and not considered a positive attribute.

He represents for us, the times when we try to fool or deceive ourselves or try to prove ourselves to others. He also symbolises the woundings caused by self-sacrifice in order to gain other's approval. He reminds you of authenticity and honouring your true nature. If you need to compromise your dreams and desires or hide yourself from someone, that person is not part of your pack. Find those that see you and receive you without judgement or condition. Also offer the same non-judgement to others, see the truth that others are, not what you want them to be, or think they should be.

Call on Lycaon when you feel shame for past actions or words and let him help you find self-forgiveness. Meet him in the mountains.

Apollo

Archetype: Bachelor Wolf
Element/s: Fire and Air
Colours: Gold and Red

Apollo is the Greek and Roman God of Light, the holy son and sun. He is also, hunter, singer, musician, poet and healer. He was born of the wolf goddess Leto and brother to Artemis the Wild Huntress and Moon Goddess. As God of music and the life-giving sun Apollo is an ally when it comes to throat chakra healing and aligning throat and crown for divine inspiration and expression. He will help with the authenticity of your voice and the creation of the song that you wish to sing or howl to the world. He is the rhythmic heart-beat of spirit and it was his long, golden hair that symbolised and contained his power and virility. He will show you how singing your true and authentic life song will bring you vitality and initiate you into your destiny, reminding you how you are the hero of your own story.

He is a bright, shining Bachelor Wolf who will teach you to honour your creations and to be creative in collaboration with the divine. Work with, or be in, sunlight together.

Cernunnos

Archetype: Grand Father Wolf
Element/s: Earth
Colours: White and Silver

Cernunnos is of one of the oldest known Celtic gods, also called The Horned One, God of beasts and the Supreme Lord of the Wildwood. Cernunnos is one of the great protectors of wolves and we can ask for his support and energy is protecting our wolves under threat on this earth. He also reminds us to rejoice in all of life and all it brings, whether good or bad. He reminds us that like wolves, we are untameable, that spark of life and elemental spirit will always reside within us, and is accessible, no matter what. Ask Cernunnos for his grounding presence when you need a reminder or affirmation that you truly do belong and that your life is as valuable as the trees, water and fire.

Call on Cernunnos as the wise and all-seeing Grand Father Wolf who nurtures and protects all life.

Loki

Archetype: He shifts between all
Element/s: Fire
Colours: Again, he shifts between all

Norse God of Trickery and Cunning. Father of the wolf children, Fenrir and Hel. Loki is well known for his wit and cleverness. He offers all a reminder not to take life too seriously, sometimes cleverness is knowing when to laugh, when to cry, when to shout and when to whisper. Every wolf is the pack knows when it is time to hunt, to defend, to watch and when it is time to play or sing. With him learn discernment. He will also teach you that both seriousness and joviality have their unique contribution, both laughter and tears are needed. Also ask Loki for a deepening of self-awareness and support with honestly acknowledging and working with one's own strengths and weaknesses. He guides the ability to shift, pivot and be adaptable.

Loki is your wolf guide when you need cunning and a different perspective or approach with a situation or dilemma. He will help you think outside of the box.

Odin

Archetype: Grand Father Wolf
Element/s: Ether and Air
Colours: White

Also known as the 'All-Father', Odin is the Norse God of Wisdom, Healing, Poetry, Magic and the Sky. Father to the Gods and the king of Valhalla, where courageous warriors who died in battle were taken. Odin will teach you about honour and respect, encouraging you to live and act with honesty to yourself and others. He also teaches about perspective, to see all and to see beyond. He is the wolf that sees in the dark and will guide you in looking past what you think you should or want to see, and see only truth. Odin asks you, what is possible beyond what you have decided or judged should be? He tells you not to act for the ego, or based simply on the conclusions of the mind. There is honour in stopping, waiting and watching before acting.

Odin is a Grand Father Wolf ready to guide you when you want to embody potentiality and need to access your deepest wisdom and knowing. Lift your head up and howl to the sky to call and honour him.

Alator

Archetype: Father Wolf
Element/s: Earth
Colours: Black and Brown

Celtic God of war and protection. His name meant both huntsman, "he who cherishes" and "he who nourishes the people". He is the Father wolf that embodies the role of hunter and provider, as well as protector of those he feeds and those he guards. He reminds you that to be able to provide for others is truly a great gift and will guide you in determining your unique strengths so that you can use them. He asks you to release any pressures you may have placed upon yourself to perfect the role of father or man. He tells you that you are enough, exactly as you are and that you are capable. Is it an invaluable offering of the masculine to create a feeling of safety, as it only when the they feel safe that the feminine and the innocent, vulnerable or young blossoms. As the wolf will bring food to his she-wolf when she is pregnant and nursing, so the masculine can also bring his consistency and reliability to the pack.

Call on Alator for grounding and his strong, solid presence. When you need to root down and work with reliability and consistency, he is your wolf guide. He will help you to build.

Charun

Archetype: Lone Wolf and Shadow Wolf
Element/s: Air and Earth
Colours: Black

The Dark Wolf, Etruscan God of the Afterlife, and Monsters. Charun symbolises our fears, worries and anxieties. He is that which we have deemed too terrifying the face, as well as the shadows that we hear whisper in the night. His mighty paw beckons you to lean closer to the dark whispers and open your ears to the below. He asks you, what if you boldly and bravely faced those shadows, looked them in the eye and stood strong, open, honest and grounded, knowing you were facing them *on purpose*? He also supports us in our fear of death and endings. He will help us come to terms with death, can be a companion in grief and will sit with us as a strong presence when we travel through the unpleasant, hard and messy stages of grief and loss. He will help you to transform pain into an opening, a rebirth. He reminds us of the necessity of the journey of death and will help you see it as a pathway to the next doorway or stage.

Courageously call on him in the night, choose to see him in the shadows. When feeling in the shadow offer him your fears, worries and anxieties to be devoured and so transmuted.

Chapter 7

The Great Wolf Fenrir

An ancient myth re-told for modern empowerment

In this chapter I offer you a re-telling, and a different perspective, on the Norse myth of Fenrir. There is so much healing and insight in this story that I invite you to approach it as a meditation or journey. Before beginning make sure that you are somewhere you won't be disturbed, maybe outside in nature, in a candlelit room, or ritual space. You may also want to take consideration of the information I shared about Fenrir in the previous chapters and listen to this at his sacred time of dusk or during the night.

Take three deep breaths with eyes closed, centre and ground, perhaps call in your wolf guides. Feel yourself present, whole and holy and ask that you receive all the codes and potentiality that is possible now to come forth from this experience.

If you would also like to hear me speaking this story you can do so on my website.

And so, we begin...

I am born of fire and ice.
I am the raging hot body of wolf.
I am the ice-cold eyes, teeth and claws of death.
I am the burning flames of creation,
I am the destruction that shatters frosty mist.
I am Fenrir,
feared and loved,
Mighty Wolf, destroyer, saviour,
Shadow and light.

I first knew that I created destruction when *they* came.

They came to our icy cave and my mother tried to defend and shield us. With ferociousness she stood before me and my siblings, her precious children, as the most powerful and strongest of Asgard came to take us away.

Her tears turned to frost, becoming patterns of destiny woven upon the shields and swords of those who feared the children of Loki and Angrboda.

My beautiful sister held my paw tight until they took me away. My claws leaving red and black marks upon her hands. Yet she smiled with knowing and reassured me "We will meet again dear brother. There is freedom, in the end".

They showed me that I was dangerous, when I looked back and saw my family torn from each other, my pack forever ripped from the safety we had taken for granted.

My fault. My nature. My punishment. My blame.

Now they have me bound, those great warriors. With dread in their eyes, they fettered and restrained me with chains. They fear me because I am unknown, different. They make me wrong.

I have great potential my mother said, "no one will ever see you Fenrir, your wolf eyes are a mirror for the darkness that lies within *them*. Yet, though this burden lies with you, so does the answer, the hope". She saw as she fed me bones and blood how they would laugh and mock at that which was frightening and would see it exiled. Yet she saw also something beyond *this* and so I stir and fight for my freedom. I want it!

As they each approach me now, I see the fear in their eyes and it feeds me. Their anger, worries, anxieties and judgements make me grow bigger and stronger. Each time they look and are faced with their own wrong, they call *me* bad. Mighty from the food of their fear, I rise and bite and struggle until my chains begin to strain and pull. And I begin to believe it each time they call me wrong, call me bad, call me dangerous.

I begin to question and curse my destiny and fate. It hurts. There is sometimes nothing but pain, a blinding combination of fire and ice, never cooling, never warming, just piercing and unrelenting and unchanging.

Yet one called Tyr comes. He comes to meet me and I see that it takes great courage. That courage begins to soothe the fear that I hold within me. I see his reflection in my eyes and he feeds me with his acknowledgement. Every time he visits, I wonder if I am not as dangerous as they have made me? I pull back my claws and rest my weary body.

Then he came, Odin, and he saw death. Then no chain was strong enough. He looked, he saw and I was so fed with fear that I felt myself grow even beyond the boundaries of my own flesh. Odin and the others watched as Tyr asked me gently to open my jaw and placed within my mouth his powerful hand. He told me his sacrifice was willingly made, offered on the altar so that I would know and remember to trust in all that is meant to be.

I did not understand until I saw them bring out what they called a silken ribbon. Yet I saw a deadly collar of barbs and spikes and it pulled tight around my neck. Down came my mighty jaw with the power of all the fears placed upon and within me. Blood flowed, the gods laughed and I felt shame.

Then at the edge of the underworld, the boundary between light and dark, I was placed. There being no room for doom in the golden halls of Asgard. I lay chained there until I knew that I was merely waiting. I waited and waited until the time came that the light began to recede and the sweet rays of the dark cast a shadow upon my chains. One by one they began to melt until my freedom was at last truth. And then I ran and ran and ran. Ran to my sister, with the memory of her blood on my paws driving me deeper and deeper into the mountains. In the centre of Hel, I found her, beautiful, radiant and as strong as I remembered.

She opens her arms and welcomes me to her home. Yes, *her* home, this place is hers and hers alone. She rules and she decides. Banishment transmuted into power. Wrong made so very right. She looks into my eyes and I see resolution, tenacity, and the grounded strength of one who has *chosen* different, rather than play victim. I see and I know it too. I lie down and rest awhile as my sister's wolves nip at the dead flesh of my wounds, stripping it away. I sleep as they lick where I was bound and their licks restore all that was broken.

When I wake, she places her hand at my neck and guides me to an underground lake. Here I look deep down into the reflection below me. I see all the fears, judgements, and conditions of other; what they have made me, what they have told me, what they chose for me. I let my grief and mourning flow as tears and sounds, into the waters, releasing hate, fear, shame, contempt, insecurity. I see all of it, not mine, none of it mine. I melt the ice and burn through all that bound and chained me.

Then, I look deeper, beyond of all of that and see, *my* eyes. I see the sun and the moon, I see the above and the below, I see ends and beginnings. I see my mother, my father, my sister, my brothers and something that is unmistakably and unapologetically me. I look and I feel the wind in my fur as I run and leap. I feel the earth beneath my paws, deep in my claws, satisfying, making my body, pulse. I feel every inch of my mighty presence, muscle to bones, blood to fur, heart to claw. *Mine*, powerful, *mine*, strong, *mine*, ferocious. Mine. I feel the chaos inside as threads to a great tapestry that will now be of my making.

I see Fenrir.
I am Fenrir.

I will bring about the end, that is the beginning.
I am death and rebirth.
I am fertile destruction and shifting foundations.
I am the dark and I am the light.
I am more and less than you can judge and decide.
I am your greatest fear and your deepest hopes.
I am the chaos and I am the resolution.
I am wolf.

Reflections on the Story of the Great Wolf

For me, Fenrir represents all that we fear within us and all that we have *made* bad, ugly and wrong about ourselves. He is a powerful representative of the shadow aspect of self, that which lies within us all. The way he is bound is the way that we lock our anxieties, worries and 'weaknesses' away. Fenrir in chains is the way that we hide or supress all of these things due to fear, shame, embarrassment or resentment.

However, binding and banishment of that which we deem unpleasant, unworthy or wrong only makes those feelings of shame or fear fester. It will grow and push at the bounds, seeking release and acknowledgement. It wants and needs to be seen and integrated, understood and addressed, turned to with compassion, not away from with disgust.

Think of what you believe to be your worst trait, the most dangerous and deadly wolf parts of you. What if you turned your eyes towards it, rather than away? What if you chose to see it, for all that it is and still offered it acceptance and understanding? What if you sought revelation there, in that 'darkness' and followed the signposts of fear, shame and worry to the truth and heart of the matter? What is the dark could be the pivotal catalyst to healing and resolution?

Like Fenrir, you are not bad, wrong or ugly. You may have believed it, you may have been told so, but it is not your intrinsic truth. The world can say what it likes but it does not change your essential nature; that are holy and that you are sacred, even when you have suffered, even when you have made mistakes, even without all the things you think you *should* have, be or know.

Some of what you deem wrong, shadow or dark within you may actually be inherited or ancestral. Part of the reason why Fenrir was feared was due to his lineage and the nature of his parents. One of the most powerful practices I share with my students is to ask yourself, what is yours, what is someone else's' and what is something else? It is truly feels like yours, then you can take responsibility for it, meet it, greet it and speak to it. If it feels like someone else's, then can you discern who, without blame or resentment? Are they any beliefs, limitations, obligations or conditions that are not yours but have been passed on down my parents, ancestors, culture or traditions? You can then remember your choice to say thank you, but no thank you! Will you be the one to finally break the bonds of these contracts or judgements and create a new world or will you keep adding to and repeating patterns of the past? It anything feels like 'something else' it may be vibration, energy or vibes that you are picking up on, or embodying, that actually belong to an event, an experience, a group of people, an idea or even place. You can return it to this place, or to source, with love and compassion, like stripping off clothes that were never yours to wear. Or there may be something that you can do to offer support, healing or compassion to that place or thing. You may have resonated with it or it called your attention to itself for a reason.

We can also apply this idea of essential sacredness to others. We must remember that no one else is essentially wrong, bad and ugly either just because they are different, make mistakes or act from a wounded place. There is much difference and diversity in the world and in nature, but it is us and us alone that makes that which is different wrong. It is a choice to see with the eyes of fear, or with the eyes of compassion, love and acceptance. It is brave to honestly and humbly acknowledge and own your fear and true courage and strength is not letting it dictate your actions nor creating further fear or discrimination from it. It is also ok that something isn't for you. Something or even someone may not resonate for you, but that doesn't make it wrong, it's just not your match. Everyone and everything fit into the puzzle somewhere.

It is the God Tyr, God of Justice, that chose to look into the eyes of the wolf and saw his own fear reflected, yet courageously chose to not let the wolf be wrong because of his fear. He knew he must offer forth his hand and that he must sacrifice his fears, his doubts and his worries on the altar of trust, so that it may be transformed into growth, opportunity, or hope.

The other Gods bound Fenrir, in an attempt to keep fear away and locked up, but each time he broke free. We try to deceive ourselves that we have no fear or pretend that we don't. We may even mock or laugh at fear but your fears are a gift, because they can show you what is important to you and what you believe is worth standing up for. For example, if you fear for the safety of your children, it will drive you to keep them from danger. If you fear the loss of your independence, it will inspire you to fight for your rights and help you in learning to honour your desires. Fear is still within the heart of the courageous warrior who fights for justice and equality yet he knows that it is not the *absence* of fear, or the wolf, that is needed, but the conscious *offering* of our fears as the tinder to the flame of our passion and purpose. It is important not to shun fear but to approach it with curiosity and compassion. Fear is not an enemy to be rid of, but your teacher. Our great challenges can become our greatest teachers. On the path of full integration every aspect of you from fear to joy, has a place and contribution. You are made of shadow and light and denial of any part of ourselves, prevents wholeness. Do not leave any part of yourself unloved, but offer yourself full acceptance, *that* is liberation.

In some stories Fenrir is banished deep into the mountain, through the cave, to the underworld, down into the land of his sister Hel. In this story I had him choosing to go there after feeling the call and a deep knowing within himself. He shared with me that in this telling he would be taking himself into death, into the shadow, into the depths of self, consciousness, and shadow to seek his healing and find his reclamation of self. In doing so he inspires you to do the same.

Whether we choose it or get taken there, we all visit the underworld in life; the dark places, the places of loss, fear, grief, anger, banishment or being lost. The underworld is a place of opportunity, the womb-tomb that is the inner portal where we can truly get to know oneself, to be with oneself in the darkest parts and see and feel fully. What did your times of darkness reveal to you about yourself, what did you see and learn there? Guaranteed you will have left a dark time or place different to how you began. You may have been left with scars but also strength and insight gained, wisdom remembered or learnt.

Fenrir invites you to go to the dark places for initiation, for threshold, with eyes and heart fully open, and to give death to those things that you are ashamed of, fear or discriminate against. Transform and transmute them into something else; trust, hope, acceptance. Weep and grieve for all that was cut away, ended, lost. See the beauty in that which was made wrong. Choose to offer love to even the 'nastiest' parts of you, then breath and choose how to rise again, fully integrated, fully knowing, claiming your path and purpose, choosing you.

Facing our fears, nightmares, demons, bad habits, grief, shame, or the things we have made wrong about ourselves, can seem like the end of the world. You may fear the destruction that may come from being truly yourself, the destruction of relationships by honouring yourself. Or it may seem overwhelming to let go of ways and ideas of being and that which was safe, comfy and known in order to come into true authenticity. Yet in the removing of our self-imposed judgements, conditions and limitations, space and opportunity are created for that which wasn't possible before.

In the ending of the old world, a new world will begin, one where you trust yourself enough to be free, where there is space for your potential and growth, where you can look into the mirror at your reflection with honesty and integrity and celebrate what is there, not what should be there.

What if the Fenrir the Wolf had not been fed fear? What if it had been fed trust, despite what was said about him? What if he had been held with compassion, instead of bound? What if he had been approached with a curiosity to truly know, rather than faced with judgement of the unknown?

What if you were to feed *yourself* only trust and acceptance, what then?

Part III

Being Wolf

Chapter 8

Tools and practices to connect with Wolf

The gaze of the wolf reaches into our soul. – Barry Lopez

Following on from all that we have explored so far in this book I would love to share with you some practical but powerful ways to connect with wolf that you can integrate into your everyday life or ritual practice. In this chapter I will cover many tools and practices and different approaches for energetic and spiritual empowerment with wolves. These offerings are inspired by the experience of my own practice and the teachings I have shared with students and clients over nearly two decades of teaching.

However, the ways to connect are as unique and diverse as you are and before we begin, I would like to remind you to follow your own intuition, always, first and foremost. Use this book as a guideline or inspiration, not as law. Use your wolf knowing to discover what resonates for you, what tools most attract you at this time and follow your instinct as to where and with what you would like to start. There are always ways to adapt practices as well, if what I share if not possible for you at this time.

Let us first start with some introductory practices and suggestions before we go on the hunt for extra layers, tools and resources to deepen your wolf ceremony, altar, practice or healing work.

INTRODUCTORY WAYS TO CONNECT TO WOLF

Here are some introductory ways to connect with the wolf essence and some tips to start you off as you begin laying some foundations for deeper work.

Physical and Emotional ways

- Engaging and reactivating the senses. Experience life through sounds, smells, sights, touch and taste, not just from your mind or thoughts. Begin by trying this when you are eating your meal, taking a walk, making love. Remember to take deep breaths, notice the colours, consciously touch the air around you, don't just taste but feel the textures, shape and vibration of foods and feel the temperature and the elements upon your skin as a conversation. Really be present to all the ways you are experiencing. You can also combine this with other tools, suggestions and journal prompts in this book, such as the howling practice, to open your senses to this experience. I also have a sensory experience audio guide for you on my website.

- Remember and honour the value of every wolf pack member and embrace your unique qualities and gift. You are a contribution exactly as you are. You came into this life with your personality and body, to have your experiences, for a reason. No one is you and that is your power. It is the same for every one of us. No one should be just a number, no one should be unloved or forgotten or made to feel ostracized. We all part of the human pack and can all contribute, and be significant in our own way. What can you do to advocate this in life and society?

- There is a small list of wolf organisations and charities at the back of this book on page, in my author note. You may want to support a wolf protection, reintroduction or conservation programme as a devotional act to the wolf essence. Some of these places offer you the opportunity to meet or witness wolves, in sanctuaries or in the wild. If you choose to go and find or be with wolves, please do so sensibly, safely and respectfully.

- Love your dog! Robert Wayne's research shows us that genetically every dog in the world can claim the wolf as its ancestor! Not that you need it, but here is an extra excuse to cuddle and spend time with your dog! Honour their lineage and ancestors, perhaps even journey and meditate with your dog (or ask someone else that is willing to share their dog). We have been companions with wolfs, wolf-dogs and then dogs for near enough 30,000 years or more! This relationship formed for mutual hunting advantage but has grown and evolved into a relationship of companionship, support, love and one of deep loyalty and devotion. What a gift! Let's share our gratitude for wolfs choice to support and love us!

- Take a walk without needing to know where you are going! Walk in the woods or forest and follow your intuition and instinct as to which direction to go, where to step and when to stop. Let your brain and thinking mind rest. Be still, breath deep and then let your heart lead you. You may alternatively want to ask your wolf guides and guardians to determine your path and destination. Invite them to go on the walk and experience it with you. While walking take notice of the colours around you, the smells, the elements, the creatures you pass, let all your senses be engaged. You may want to stop and paint or journal what you see, feel, smell or add your own intuitive sounds or song as an offering to nature.

- Take part in team activities, sport or creative ventures. Play is vitally important to the wolf pack as it aids in learning social and hunting skills as well as family bonding and contentment. Team or group socialising, fun and play can also support you in experiencing the same strengthening of bonds with those around you and practising communication. Vary your socialising and add diversity so you can develop your empathy and understanding of all ages, genders, cultures and religions. In the wolf pack all offer joy and learning opportunities to each other, the old play with young, parents with children and siblings. Even if you feel you most relate to the lone wolf or lone wolf stage, find a way to create deeply nourishing companionship. Notice what you can learn from others and seek the value in everyone.

Spiritual Ways

- In your rituals or activities bring speech or song into your work, therefore opening the throat chakra, and activating the voice to express what you need to speak or sound. Deeply *feel* your words. Practice expression and communication that rises up from your grounded roots, up through the heart to check for alignment and truth, and then out, clear and honestly.

- Howl if you to need to. Find a place and a way that is comfortable for you. Growl and bark, opening in a way that can tone or express what is held deepest within you. If you can, do this as close as you can to the ground, let her hold you, support you. Try having your feet barefoot on the ground or lying down. If you find you have excess energy that you need to move, then physical movement can be helpful. Dance, run, jump or shake with your howling and growling.

  If you are worried about being heard or disturbing others, do this into a cushion, in the woods or I have even experienced many a vocal healing and clearing in my car! Check in with yourself whether you need to do this alone or with support. Sometimes it is space alone and away from things that we need. If so, honour that. However, sometimes taking ourselves away or doing things alone, can be running away or hiding. Shame or embarrassment can be huge obstacles to healing, especially with self-expression. My advice? Do it anyway, even if you feel embarrassed, even if you feel silly. Just because you feel silly, it doesn't mean that that is the reality. Do it, for you and your healing, and be courageous wolf. If you don't want to, do not let yourself go through this alone, let a pack of loving supporters be there for you and with you. I facilitate this type of healing facilitation in my coaching, courses and retreats.

- The colours of root chakra red and browns, blues for throat, yellow and golds for solar plexus can be worn in your clothes or adornment to embody the energetic vibrations of wolf themes in connection to the chakras (energetic centres of the body). Or use black, grey, white or red to symbolise different wolf archetypes or energy. You could also use these colours in your art, food, drinks, your altar space or flowers.

- Begin with wolf meditations and journeys to meet you your wolf guides and guardians and during these encounters ask their advice and guidance for further exploration and learning. Still and moving meditations are both ok, with my students we use both dance meditations with wolves and meditative journeys while seated. To meditate with wolves just find yourself in a relaxed, comfortable place, close your eyes and take some deep breaths. Ask them to come forward into your space or mind's eyes. They will often meet you at threshold places, such as the edge of the forest, river or cave entrance. It is then your choice as to whether you travel deeper into other places with them. Do this in a place and time you won't be disturbed, but feel safe. I have many free introductory meditations you can use on my website, YouTube and SoundCloud.

- Use the wolf affirmations that are included in the pack of this book to remind yourself daily of the wolf energy or characteristics you which to embody or emulate. Use them to focus your body and intention. You could place them on the fridge, the mirror or where you work out or bathe. You can turn the affirmations into pieces of art or say them when you take a flower essence formula, anointing oil or hold a wolf themed crystal. Another idea is also to record yourself saying them and play it back to yourself, while you sleep or mediate.

DEEPENING YOUR PRACTICE

Here are further sacred tools, places and times for deepening your Wolf connection, facilitating wolf empowerment and creating ritual.

It is important for us to give just as much as we take from wolf essence and spirit. Like a mamma wolf your pack of guides and guardians will watch you and guide you, hunt out that which you seek and bring home your healing, remembrance and empowerment. In return we can offer them our presence and our gratitude but also offerings in the form of ritual, time, ceremony and intentional communion.

Approach all of these activities and suggestions with honour, reverence and gratitude to Wolf. In the end it's not so much *what* you bring, it's *how* you bring it that is important. May this be just the beginning of creating sacred and holy communion, and a deepening of a relationship of reciprocity that benefits both yourself, wolf essence and humanity!

SACRED TIME

Here are some times that you may wish to mark as a good opportunity to connect with wolf essence or create a ritual or ceremony.

Wolf Moon – The Wolf Moon is in January and is the first full moon of the calendar year. It was called the Wolf Moon as wolves were heard communicating with more frequency as they hunted in the scarcest time of the year. A full moon in the dead of winter, it signifies a time for transformation, forgiveness and reflection. This is a really great time to meditate or enjoy a journey or visualisation with your wolf guides. You have several recorded audio journey with wolves on my website that you can enjoy during this full moon.

Lupercalia – The portal is open 13th to 15th February, with the high energy point on the 14th February – Lupercalia is the Ancient Roman Wolf Festival, particularly connected with the She-Wolf of Rome, Lupa. You can find out much more about Lupa, Lupercalia and how to celebrate both in more detail in my book *Lupa. She-Wolf of Rome and Mother of Destiny.*
January to February is a general mating season for wild wolves. You could perhaps use this time to call in a mate into your life if desired or to explore your own inner divine marriage.

1st February – Feast Day of Brigid/ Birgit, Wolf Goddess and Queen. Connect into the fires of creation and the elemental wolves of Fire around Imbolc. You may be a wolf that is seeking to initiate a project, business or journey and this is a great time to utilise your passion and procreative energy to cross the threshold of beginning anew!

Festivals of Wolf God Mars – The sacred months of October and also March, which is named in honour of him. Celebrate and connect to him, or the archetype of Father Wolf all month long.

March 1st – Feast Day of Mars Pater, Mars the Father, when the Roman troops and people celebrated the birthday of the God Mars. Connect this day with Father Wolf or Alpha Wolf.

Mars Invictus – 14th May – The Roman festival of Mars Invictus (for whom there was a temple dedicated to in Rome), meaning the "Unconquered Mars" is a potent time to connect into your warrior aspect within. Spend some time aligning with and getting clear on your purpose, skills and knowledge and how you can best serve the world. It would be great day to set intentions for a particular project or cause that you wish Mars's fire to ignite and amplify.

1st September – Feast Day of Cernunnos, Grand Father Wolf and Lord of the Wildwood. Use this day to give thanks to Cernunnos for his protection of the forests and of nature. Ask, or give offering, for his continued guardianship of Wolf. You may want to visit or walk with him in the woods or forest or create something for nature's benefit.

November – 6th November was considered the birth day of Artemis, while Apollo's was the 7th November. Celebrate and honour the twins and their wolf goddess Mother Leto on these two days. Use it as a day of reflection on all that you have birthed and brought forth throughout the year and give thanks. You can also use these days to connect to Mother Wolf and Maiden, Bachelor Wolf.

Feast of Jól (or known now as Yule) – Mid-Winter/ end of December – Festival celebrated by Germanic and Norse people that was connected to Wolf God Odin and associated with the Wild, untamed part of the year and the time of Hunting. Connect to Grand Father Wolf at this time and connect into your inner wisdom.

Archetypal times to connect to particular pack themes

Autumn – Time of the lone wolf. This is the time that lone wolves generally have emigrated from the pack and are roaming. It is a time of searching, hunting and aligning, more often as individual wolves, rather than as a pack. Also, a time of release and focusing on individual reflection. What have you learnt this year and what are you preparing to leave behind, or hoping to repair or incubate in the coming winter?

Winter – Time of the Wolf Mother. When the she-wolves generally mate, then create their dens and go through pregnancy (ready to birth in early spring). A time of incubation, reflection and planting the seeds. Also, for the pack a time of searching and seeking, as the pack hunt together to ensure more food is found for mum and pups. So, a time of coming together in mutual support.

Spring – Time of the birth of pups. In this period life is centred around the den. It is a time of teaching and tending the young and so a potent time to work with the energy of the wolf pup.

It is a time of learning as well as a time of emerging and of tending the shoots from that which you planted in winter. What is beginning for you, what intentions are you beginning to nurture and hope to see grow?

Summer – Archetypal time for warrior and his/her creation-action energy. The wolf pack is exploring, hunting, playing and growing. This is the time to enjoy community and being with your pack, exploring the land, life and each other. This is when the pack is at his highest number of members. There are many mouths to feed, so this is a time of team building and team work. Explore what it means to be offer yourself on behalf of a greater cause.

Sacred Time Activity

Full Wolf Moon Ritual for Empowerment

This ritual is for you to connect with the energy of the moon and ask it to facilitate a wolf empowerment ritual. The full moon is a time of abundance and of fullness and so it is a potent time to ask, seek or manifest the amplification or expansion of an energy, intention or essence.

Conduct this ritual anytime during the night of the full moon, in particular the 3-hour portal leading up to the full moon, when the moon is still waxing (after the full moon peak, the moon will begin to wane, so the day or hours after will change to become the energy of release or turning in, rather than amplification).

1. Begin by gathering your favourite wolf crystals, images, talismans, herbs or sacred objects that you wish to charge in the moonlight.
2. Then think of a personal strength that you have, wish for or want to amplify and write it down on a piece of

paper. (Examples: Courage, Kindness, Enthusiasm, Trustworthiness, Creativity, Patience, Respectfulness, Determination, Dedication).

3. Take the piece of paper and any other items out into the moonlight. You may want to place them on the ground, in a bowl, a sacred place or somewhere safe from being trampled or moved.
4. Take three deep breaths. You may want to call in your wolf guides as you place your objects. You can also at this point use any of the invocations or affirmations suggested in this book, or use the one I have recorded for you, to follow along with.
5. Stay with all of these offerings for a while and allow yourself to feel connected to the wolf strength you wish to align with. Feel the earth power running up your legs into you roots and know that you are powerful, grounded and connected. Hear your wolves howling.
6. Keep in your mind's eye on that intention you wrote down, that something you want to work on becoming stronger. Envision yourself as having achieved that, or already embodying it. What would it feel like to know, hold and be that strength? Where do you feel the power in your body? What would it create?
7. Take some time to sit, breath, walk or dance with these questions. Ask your wolf guides and guardians to guide and support you in the creation of that which you desire. Perhaps repeat the strength a few times, or speak it out loud. Then leave the items and the piece of paper out in the moonlight to charge in the moon rays.
8. Retrieve the items after your dance, meditation or journalling or after a few hours. Intuitively feel when it is time. If you wish to leave it overnight, I would recommend doing so the night before the full moon, when the moon

is waxing (to avoid spilling into the waning phase). Also be aware that unless it is your intent to solar-infuse the items as well, then take them in before the sun is fully risen. Your items and paper will have been charged by the moonlight and you can add them to your altar or journal for further work or as a reminder to daily revisit your desires and intent.

9. Make note of your thoughts and dreams that night or day and see what further insight and wisdom comes through.

Know that even if you can't see the moon, or if it is cloudy that the rays of the moon will be present in the night sky and will work their magic!

SACRED TOOLS

Sacred Colours

Grey, Brown, Red, White, Black, Gold and Blue – Use any of these in your work with wolves, whether you wear the colours, paint with them or add them to sacred spaces or adornment.

A note on colour

You will find that there are grey, brown, white, red and black wolves that roam this earth, all variations within the two species of wolf; grey and red. Sometimes the colouring is due to context and place, such as wolves are generally whiter in places that have more snow. Grey wolves are the most common in Europe and red wolves are the closest wolves to extinction with very few left in the wild. Arabian, Eastern, Indian wolves as mentioned are all smaller and generally sandier coloured than the Grey Wolf, looking more similar to domestic dogs.

As wolves age their fur can also gradually get lighter, with some grey wolves becoming almost completely white and black wolves becoming light grey. Each time their fur moults it will change slightly in shade.

As for deities from mythology and historic remains it seems that there is just as much variety. In general, the ancient considered the Morrigan's wolf to be a white or white and red wolf, yet archetypally she also connects to the colour black. Mars's wolves appear as black, just as Fenrir was said to be a black wolf. Lupa appears generally as grey-white or white and Odin's wolves are also described as grey but archetypally his wolves can also manifest as white. In both Welsh and Irish mythology, white or white and red denoted an animal of having otherworldly origins, whereas in others cultures black denoted the same. Both white and black has been associated with death or life in different cultures.

If a wolf appears to you in dreams, visualisations their colours might not fit into these boxes, so just be open to whatever manifests for you. Sometimes there is deeper meaning in the colours that they choose to appear as, the colour might be a message itself or an indication as to whom the wolf is representing. Colour is energetic, as well as literal and be aware that outside the realms of physicality colour can be more fluid and less defined.

As mentioned before wolves have also often appeared as blue or with a blue aura reflecting wolf energy and its connection to throat chakra or blue healing vibrations. Gold can denote a wolf that has particular connections to sovereignty, queenship and royal lineage.

Colour can also be, just that, solely colour, with no more depth and meaning than the fact that the wolf is appearing as such, perhaps just for the joy of it or they know you'll like or recognise it!

Let your inner knowing be your guide, or ask your wolf directly if their colour is an important message or sign for you.

Stones, gems and crystals to work with the wolf archetypes and themes:

For cleansing, protection and grounding:
Black tourmaline, amethyst and labradorite
For connection to intuition:
Shungite, black malachite, garnet, howlite, black moonstone
For confidence and self-assurance:
Tiger's eye, green jade, rose quartz, green aventurine
For communication and expression:
Lapis lazuli, aquamarine, amazonite, blue apatite

Essential Oils/ Incense

Please use a base oil if you intend to use any of these essential oils on the skin. For an oil burner add 6 drops of each oil to the water.

Cedarwood – for grounding, strengthening the inner pillar and root chakra clearing.

Pine – for healing or empowering the masculine. It also provides energetic protection and strengthens boundaries

Eucalyptus/Peppermint – for opening and healing the throat chakra and clarity of voice.

Sandalwood – For heart chakra healing, activation as well as awareness and release.

Flower, Tree & Crystal Essences

2-3 drops directly on your tongue or skin, or into a glass of water or bath.

3 drops, 3 times a day if using as a formula.

Marigold Flower Essence – for speaking your truth and empowering your voice.

Borage Flower Essence – for courage and boosting self-belief.

St Johns Wart Flower Essence – for being fully incarnated in your body, feeling safe to be embodied.

Olive Tree Essence – for embodying your inner king and to support you in honouring your inner authority.

Topaz Gem Essence – for self-confidence, greater perspective and invoking the will to be patience and persistence.

Sacred numbers

42 (number of teeth)

9 (days of labour, wolf pups are nursed for approx. 9 weeks and 9 is also the average oldest age for a wild wolf)

12 (average oldest age for wolf in captivity and the average number of a pack)

63 (day pregnancy)

Howling can be heard in forested areas for up to 6.6 miles and in open areas 9.6 miles.

Scent marks are always approximately 240 metres apart in boundary routes.

Interestingly all of these numbers are connected to the sacred number 3, the number of the triple goddess, triskele and the three worlds.

Primary Related chakras

Root Chakra – For themes of safety, the pack, home, belonging, grounding, sexuality.

Solar Plexus Chakra – For themes of empowerment, personal identity, confidence, self-belief.

Throat Chakra – For healing wounding of the voice or expression and themes of communication and relating.

Some wolves may work with a specific energy or can support you with a particular chakra healing. An example of this is that Grand Mother and Grand Father Wolf are particularly supportive with root and crown chakra work (nurturing, belonging and healing wounds around the home). Also, the she-wolves can also support you in actively working with the sacral chakra (creating, birthing, creative expression, emotions), father wolves with solar plexus (personal power and self-authority) and alpha wolves with the throat (communication and expression). It does not matter whether you work with the Celtic or Vedic chakra system, both are applicable.

Astrology

Connect or meditate with:

1. The constellation of Lupus, meaning 'the wolf' in Latin.
Lupus was first noted by the Greek astronomer Ptolemy in the 2nd century. Also known as Therium, meaning 'wild animal', to the ancient Greeks and Bestia, 'the beast', to the ancient Romans. This constellation holds the origin of wolf essence, energy, lineage and ancestry. Locate and meditate with the brightest star in the constellation called Alpha Lupi, to connect to the ancestral alpha energy. It shines a powerful blue.

2. The constellations of Canis Major and Canis Minor.
Canis Major and Minor are constellations powerful for connecting to any of the Canis family; wolves, dogs, jackals, coyote. In particular connect to the Dog Star Sirius, the brightest star in the night sky, who name means 'glowing'. Sirius is also connected with Goddesses such as Isis and Inanna, Goddesses of Motherhood, fertility and War who were depicted accompanied by wolves or dogs.

3. Planets.

There are also specific planets that connect to certain wolf deities. For example, the God Mars with the planet Mars, Hel and Fenrir with Pluto, Apollo with the Sun, Diana with the crescent moon. The planet Mercury is also a powerful planet to work with along the wolf themes of communication, expression and memory, as well as boundaries and being adaptable. Saturn can support you with structure and discipline, teaching you wolf tenacity, determination and stamina.

Elements

Primary – Element of Earth

Forest and Plains wolves are potent allies in connecting to the earth element and are guardians of earth.

Secondary – Water

Coastal wolves are connected to both the elements of water and earth as they live at the intersection of land and sea.

(See also elemental wolves and archetypal elements in Chapter 4.)

Allies

Raven/ Crow – In the physical realms Wolf and Raven have a sacred relationship of practicality but also friendship and are often found together playing and feeding. This allyship also transfers into the spiritual realms. Together they can support you with the exploration and dissection of your shadow self, or inner world so you can gain greater wisdom and understanding of self. The wolves will support you in the seeking, finding and listening within your inner realms and the raven/crow in the taking apart of conditions, judgements and limitations or alternatively the assembling of parts and ideas.

Stag, Boar and Bear – When these four work together it is like being in the presence of the high council of elders, an unparalleled unity of the oldest and wisest ones! For our ancestors these four pillars of the forest were symbols of sovereignty and guardianship, as well as the otherworld and the divine. These lords and ladies of the forest will all support you in working with and exploring your wild self as sacred, and reclaiming your self-authority and inner strength.

Snake – The snake appears very often in shared symbology or mythology of many wolf gods and goddesses, such as Cernunnos, Fenrir, Odin and Leto. Both snake and wolf are connected to the element of earth and earth themes and will support you in connecting to and healing your root chakra. Like the wolf the snake is also a fierce protector, as personified by its venom and it is, also like wolf, a symbolic vehicle to the afterlife, through the shedding of its skin. Call on wolf and snake in union for exploration of any of these themes.

Sacred items you may want to add to your altar or ritual:

- Soil and earth – bring the element of earth into your space, ritual or altar. You may want to use soil, earth, leaves or a stone from somewhere that you call home and reminds you of belonging.
- Water – to represent river, lake or sea, especially if any of bodies of water links symbolically with your wolf (for example, coastal wolves, or there is water in their mythological story). You may want to place this in a sacred bowl or chalice.
- Teeth or bones – a symbolic reminder of bone deep wisdom, ancestors, strength, legacy and, or death (environmentally friendly and sustainably sourced)
- Sticks – a favourite toy of younger wolves can be a

reminder of play, fun, direction, ingenuity and learning as well as wolf pup energy.
- The wolf colours of black, white, grey, brown or red. Dependant on the spiritual wolf archetype you want to connect with, deity or guide you wish to honour.
- A Wolf Flower Essence Formula, such as the one I supply that brings in all of the tree and flower essences that align with and offer the healing of wolf essence.
- A cloak or shawl wrapped around you can represent the cave or the womb if you are connecting with the themes of the den, womb-tomb, winter time or mother and grandmother wolf energy or archetype.
- Any of the essential oils and crystals mentioned previously.

I also have specific wolf deity altar item recommendations for many wolf gods and goddesses such as Lupa, Mars, Hel, Apollo, Morrigan and Odin on my YouTube channel.

Offerings of blood and milk

Milk – Often ewe's or goat's milk was used in ancient wolf themed rituals, representing the nurturing nature of mother wolf to her pups and the breastmilk of the goddess herself, as well as the wisdom/life received by the participant from the divine. You can take milk to your altar, drink it in ceremony or give some back to the earth. Women could also use or offer some of their breastmilk in their rituals as representative of the milk of the goddess.

Blood – Symbolic of life, vitality, creation, lineage and ancestry. In the past, such as in the festival of Lupercalia, the blood of sacrificed animals was used to anoint or smear those involved in wolf initiations, ritual and ceremony. In the Lupercalia it was smeared upon the forehead, or third eye, as a reminder of the sacrifice of illusion and judgement in order to be able to then see clearly. Like milk, this offering was most often the blood of a goat.

In my personal opinion, animal sacrifice is not compassionate practice, nor is it at all necessary. As we have moved now into the conceptual age the divine has indicated a move away from the sacrificial death of physical beings, such as animals, humans etc. to instead offering a sacrifice of your old and outdated ways of being, unhealthy or limiting emotions and habits. Sacrifice your regret, your shame, any feelings of lack or self-doubt. So, perhaps instead of, or symbolic of, a blood sacrifice you could write in red that which you are offering from within yourself as sacrifice upon the altar of transformation e.g., fear, resentment, nail biting, procrastination etc.

I also invite women to engage with the menstrual mysteries and to use their monthly blood as offering to the earth, as a symbolic release of cycles, or the past and in reverence to the sacred and holy that is our bodies and womb. You can add your menstrual blood to the altar as the most holy of liquids, the elixir of creation.

Wine, red berries and fruits and red cloth or ribbon are also good alternatives, that can be symbolic of blood.

Talismans

It is because of the qualities of wolf essence that many approach wolf energy, deity or archetype in order to achieve or manifest that essence. There is an awareness of and attraction to the potentiality of these characteristics and so we seek to embody or emulate through archetype or energy. Totem, emblem, or talisman can serve as a reminder or a reinforcement of intent, purpose and communion around that which we wish to emulate, manifest or be inspired by.

Throughout history tribes, families, cities and countries acquired animal totems, sometimes in remembrance of a famous ancestor and their exploits or because of an affinity with a local animal or again the characteristics of that animal or its association with a deity. In times past these totem animals found their ways onto battle standards and heraldry and often had an accompanying motto. In heraldry the wolf generally represented a noble and courageous character and symbolised dedication and perseverance.

Here are some ideas for various totem's, emblems and talismans that symbolise that particular essence of wolf that you may want to have with you, to wear, add to your altar, body art or take on a journey or training course. I invite you to create your own ceremony when adding intent to these talismans. Create sacred space and time, call in a guide and or the elements and imbue the token with your desired characteristics or intention.

Wolf's tooth Talisman

A wolf's bite is five times stronger than a human and a wolf tooth talisman can serve as reminder of the potential power of communication. Worn around the neck is can support you in the discernment of your words and thoughts; are they helpful, what is your true intention and are you speaking with authenticity and respect of ourself and others.

Crystals

You may also want to create a wolf talisman using crystals. I would recommend black Tourmaline and, or Labradorite.

Wolf figures

You may want to consider the symbology and energy behind the imagery of wolf, if you are to use of a wolf statue or wolf depiction as a talisman. In this way the Talisman may be statue, necklace, tattoo or altar piece. If you are drawn to one of these images, or find a wolf that calls to you in any of these depictions, take it as a sign to work deeper with that energy!

- *Howling Wolf* – Look for, or create images of the wolf howling, head reaching up to the sky, moon, stars or forest, perhaps with mouth open. Howling wolf will inspire you to confidently and considerately communicate your truth and wisdom and connect with your unique expression.
- *Running Wolf* – Look for, or create images of the wolf in motion, elemental and wild. The running wolf will remind you of freedom and the importance of taking aligned and purposeful action. Also, a good talisman if you are searching for something, whether it be self, a partner or a job. It is the energy of moving *towards*.
- *Seated Wolf* – Look for, or create images of the wolf that is seated but not howling. The wise wolf sits, waits, considers and takes all in. Seated Wolf will inspire you to reflect, connect, contemplate or consider deeply before, or after you act, speak or create.
- *Mother Wolf* – Look for, or create images of the wolf with her cubs. She is the mother wolf that embodies fierce maternal love and protection and will support you in offering this for yourself or others. This is a great talisman to have on a necklace, to keep close to your heart.
- *Sleeping Wolf* – Look for, or create images of the wolf that sleeps or rests, perhaps lying down. A reminder that there is a time for rest, retreat, to be within and explore the internal or otherworld realms. You may want to have this talisman in a place that you consider your nest or den, that you go to for time out or inner work. A talisman for dream work.

Food, Teas and Herbs

Herbs

These herbs particularly align with the themes, healing and wisdom of wolf. Use these herbs as ceremonial/altar offerings, in a ritual bath or in a cleansing stick. You could also explore, with an herbal practitioner, their uses as medicinal tinctures on your healing journey with wolf.

Rosemary
Cardamon
Fennel
Cinnamon
Liquorice

Tea blend

For Grounding and Nourishing your roots and soothing and clearing the throat chakra.

Ginger root
Liquorice root
Aniseed
Cinnamon Bark
Vervain Leaf
Coriander

Please seek advice from a medical herbalist if you are unsure as to the suitability of any herbs in relation to a health conditions or medications.

A note on eating bones.

There was one time when I was in that half dreaming space in the early hours of the morning and it was during a hot time of summer. On sticking one leg out from under the duvet, I felt a chuckle coming from some of my wolf guardians who commented that my leg looked like a succulent and rather tasty lamb chop.

The humour of my guides aside, on a serious note, one aspect of working with wolves is that often while embodying their energy you become deeply in touch with your bodies needs and instincts. While I am working deeply with my wolf guides, I find that I have very strong cravings for bones. Wolves remind me of a bone deep need for building strength in my physical body and supporting nutritionally my body structures. For some of you this craving may be easy to remedy and you are happy to sit gnawing on bones. However, for those of you that crave something alternative to deeply nourish your mind, body and soul I wish to share with you below some recipes for Bone Broth from my Ayurveda teacher, Talya. The vegan bone broth for me has not only been a life-saver when I've been craving bones, but also has been incredibly healing in general. As well as immune boosting, it is also highly nourishing and super yummy. Here are her two recipes for a chicken and vegan bone broth.[17] Drink once daily or more often when you need some deep nourishment or healing. It can also be used as a liquid base for your general cooking. The recipe uses US measurements.

Bone broth Recipes

Talya's Chicken Bone Broth

Preparation Time: 15 minutes, plus 18 to 24 hours cooking time
Yield: 1 gallon

One whole organic roasted chicken, deboned
2 pounds organic chicken backs (available from the butcher at most health food stores and farmer's markets)

1 pound of organic chicken feet, optional
22 cups water
2 strips kombu
2 Tablespoons apple cider vinegar
1 teaspoon salt
1 yellow onion, roughly chopped
8 garlic cloves, smashed
2-inches fresh ginger root, sliced
1 teaspoon ground cumin
1 teaspoon ground turmeric
½ teaspoon asafetida
4 Bay Leaves
1 bunch bok choy or celery, roughly chopped

Remove the meat from the roasted chicken and set aside. In a large, 6 to 8-quart stock pot over medium-high heat, add the roasted chicken bones, chicken backs, chicken feet, water, kombu, apple cider vinegar and salt. As you bring the water to a boil, add the remaining ingredients.

Bring to a boil and reduce the heat to simmer. Simmer for a full 18 to 24 hours. Remove from heat. Strain and store in ½-gallon mason jars. Leave a few inches of space at the top of each jar. Allow the broth to cool completely before refrigerating or freezing. Refrigerated bone broth will stay good for 5 to 7 days.

How To Serve: Pour 16-ounces into your favourite mug. Stir in 1 teaspoon ghee, 1 teaspoon coconut oil, ½ teaspoon apple cider vinegar, salt to taste and juice of ½ lemon.

Talya's Vegan "Bone" Broth

Preparation time: 1 hour
Yield: 6 servings

¼ Cup Wakame (sea vegetable)
4 Tablespoons of Coconut Oil
2 cups of celery, chopped
½-inch fresh turmeric root, finely chopped (optional)
1 inch of fresh ginger root, finely chopped
2 garlic cloves, finely minced
2 bay leaves
1 cup of golden beets, sliced thin
12 cups of low/no sodium vegetable broth / water
2 tablespoons of coconut aminos
¼ cup of miso paste
2 cups of spinach, roughly chopped
2 cups of kale, roughly chopped
¼ cup of parsley or arugula, roughly chopped

Soak the Wakame in one cup of water and set aside.

In a large stock pot, sauté the celery in coconut oil over a low to medium heat. Add the optional turmeric, ginger and garlic; sauté for 5 minutes, or until the celery in tender. Add the bay leaves and the beets to the celery. Pour in the vegetable broth and the coconut aminos. Increase the heat to medium. Pour in the wakame and its soak water. Cover. Bring the broth to a near boil, then reduce the heat to low. Allow it to simmer for 45minutes. Remove from the heat. Stir in the miso paste until it dissolves. Add the spinach, kale and parsley and let it sit, covered for another 10 minutes. This recipe can also be made in a slow cooker or crockpot set on low-medium heat for 4 hours

How To Serve: Pour 16-ounces into your favourite mug. Stir in 1 teaspoon ghee, 1 teaspoon coconut oil, ½ teaspoon apple cider vinegar, salt to taste and juice of ½ lemon.

A WOLF WAY OF LIFE

Wolves' live life fully, primal and wild with the innate knowing that they are in and of nature, not separate from, or controller of. This is in contrast to our often disconnected and detached human way of living. Therefore, they offer you valuable guidance in living, fully embodied as a physical, earth being. Wolf will undoubtably encourage you to get in touch with your body, to nurture it and enjoy it.

They spent a lot of their time running and hunting as well as playing and often when connecting to the wolves you may feel a desire to use your body in ways that keep it both active and healthy. Wolves have powerful bodies and are built for stamina and speed. Generally, when working with them there can be also be present a restless or powerfully motivating energy within you that is channelled from, or inspired by wolf.

Some fitness and physical activities that the Wolf can draw you to are:

- weight lifting and resistance training
- mountain/forest walking,
- running and jumping
- swimming

Sometimes you may find the wolves even call you *because* your physical body is in need of movement or strengthening! Wolf can be a messenger from the divine that is telling you to get fit, get healthy and to treat your body with respect and reverence and nourish it with pleasurable food and activity.

If the activities aren't possible for you then do not worry! I am a dancer and have taught sacred and ritual dance for two decades and the wolves love it when I dance. They enjoy joining in and leaping about around me! So, if weights or running really isn't for you, there will be other ways to get your body moving, even ones that can be done seated – ask your wolf guides for further guidance or ideas.

You may also want to spend more unstructured time outside. Get in nature as often as you can and just explore and open to connection and guidance. The most precious time we can actually spend is that which is without the objectives or conditions of the mind but free and playful time led by the heart.

Intuitive eating

In my coaching and courses with my students I share about the importance of intuitive eating and listening to your body, first and foremost when it comes to food. Our wolf guardians and guides can help us with this! When fully immersing in the embodiment of any archetype, sometimes their lifestyle is something we may want to experience. Food consumption and exercise may be an aspect of this.

When channelling or emulating wolf energy and archetype you may feel the impulsive need for running, playfulness, eating raw steak and bone munching. You may alternatively find that your body wants to engage deeper with earth's medicine through using solely herbs and plants only. With the wolf pup archetype and energy, you may feel drawn to exploring and experimenting with food, maybe curiously trying many different things and ways of eating. Mother Wolf would be fantastic for finding foods, drinks and ways of eating that suit your body type or constitution. You may also need to find the stillness and grounding of meal time or tea meditation with Grand Father wolf if you have been too busy or feeling burnt out!

Either way, Wolf reminds you that you are the authority of your body, and only you can say what is right for you. Start with listening to your body, then listen deeper, and then deeper again. Your body knows what it needs, and it changes daily. Consistently check in with your body, show up for it, honour it, respect it. The latest fad or diet trend cannot do that, they are always too general and never personalised. Whatever it is that *you* need to keep yourself nourished and healthy, as much as you can, choose ways and resources that are sustainable, respectful and compassionate to both you and to the earth that provides for and supports you!

I think one of the ways you can most honour wolf is to pay the upmost respect and offer guardianship of the land and earth. Wolves live sustainably, only eating and using what they need, as well as collaborating with other species, such as raven and bear, by sharing resources and prey. The decline and extinction of wolves in many areas is primarily due to human destruction of not just the wolf, but also its habitat and natural prey for our own over consumption, greed and selfishness. It is our responsibility as humans to be dedicated and considerate stewards of the earth and wolf will guide you as to how you can uniquely and compassionately contribute in all ways of being and living.

Nap time!

As a crepuscular species, wolves tend to spend the middle of the day resting and regaining energy. This means that they're then ready to frolic and explore just a few hours later! Wolves are highly proficient at afternoon naps so follow their example, nap when you need to, there is no shame at all in resting and resting is just as productive as action.

Rest to restore, rest to fill up, rest to heal, rest for fun!

Creation of boundaries

Wolves are very effective as establishing and expressing clearly their boundaries and will act as protectors and guardians of your space as well as empowering and teaching you to also do the same for yourself. There may be many times in your life you need to establish, affirm, strengthen or even dissolve boundaries, whether they be around your needs, desires, space, home, or body.

Even your business and creative activities are an extension of your spiritual devotions and so need to be set up with strong energetic and spiritual boundaries. Remember always to align your boundaries with the highest and most holy intent and purpose. Ask for them to be healthy and to support you. Also re-read the notes in the first chapter of this book on boundaries as a reminder of when, how and why to make them or dissolve them.

Symbolic boundary

If you have an altar and sacred space, a home or someone for whom you wish to establish as a holy and protected place then you can ask the wolves to mark that territory with you. Just as they would in the wild with their territory invite them to walk with you and with your steps together mark the edges of the boundary you wish to create. You can add cleansing herbs, or essences to this ritual if you wish as well. However, it is enough to just walk the path with your wolf guardians asking them to guard it with their energy, perhaps visualising them standing around the edges. Set your intentions as you make this walk, aligning them with your truth, using discernment and intuition to check in with what is truly needed or necessary at this time. The wolves will keep guard if this boundary truly supports you, they know when something is needed and trust that they will know if you are feeling fearful, vulnerable or just in need of some extra oomph!

Revisit and repeat the walk of these boundaries with your wolves to frequently check in with whether they need updating, expanding, closing down or re-enforcing. Re-align with the intent of that boundary and also see if it has matured or is still relevant. If you close down a boundary, give thanks to your wolf guardians and let them know that their support in this way and this place is no longer needed. Be sure to release them with respect and gratitude.

Energetic personal boundary

A very simple but effective way to create a boundary around yourself is to spend five minutes every morning visualising this boundary around you. You can imagine it as anything from light, to a fence, a duvet, a lake of water or a forest. Feel it or ask it to surround you front, back, side to side, above and below. Ask for anything that is not yours and does not belong to you to return to source with love and compassion. Then ask your wolf guides to sit guardian around your boundary only allowing in that which you choose or that which supports your highest purpose and path.

Again, I have guided boundary creation meditations on my YouTube channel and in my courses that you can use.

Physical boundary

If appropriate or physically possible you may want to create an actual boundary, with a frequently walked pathway, such as wolves use, made clear with footprints, or natural produce such as gravel, stones or wood.

Upon an altar or inside space you may want to draw a boundary with stones, crystals, soil, earth, sticks or leaves. You can also use any of the wolf themed flower essences or crystals previously suggested.

Menstruating women may also want to use their sacred menstrual blood as a boundary marker. As one of the most holy fluids on this planet it is a truly powerful offering to place on behalf of personal boundaries and mother wolf in particular will support you with placing this offering on the earth.

For the creation of this boundary use the same procedure as the symbolic boundary but re-enforce it will physical markers.

Throat Chakra Healing

Wolves are the most powerful allies when it comes to working with the throat chakra and this focus may come up a lot when you are embodying or healing with Wolf. The throat chakra is our energetic centre for communication and expression. It swirls with beautiful shades of blue and you will find when working with wolf energy that the energy and auras of Wolf is often vivid with these shades of blue. Anytime that you are working with wolves on the themes of communication, self-expression or with the throat chakra you may want to:

- Wear or use the colour blue in decoration or adornment.
- use the essential oils Eucalyptus, Peppermint and Frankincense.
- Use the crystals Amazonite and Lapis Lazuli.
- use marigold or garden pea flower essence. Also, Emerald gem essence.
- Connect to the element of air and the elemental air wolves
- Explore sound through singing, gibberish, rhetoric or wolf noises such as howling
- Use somatic dance and focus specifically on chest, shoulder and head movements

In the next chapter of this book, I also have a Wolf throat chakra invocation that you may want to utilise during ceremony, practice or healing sessions. Use this in combination with any of the above tools. I do so with clients in sounding sessions and is helps to amplify the intention and healing.

Working with wolves and the throat chakra will help you to clarify and strengthen your communication and expression.

Reflect on all that you have learnt about wolf communication and the way they use different howls or vocalisations and how it resonated with your own throat chakra. What woundings around your throat chakra would benefit from exploring this work deeper? What came up in the journal prompts in chapter 1 that you want to take away now and begin a healing journey accompanied by all of the tools above supporting you?

Also don't forget how the throat chakra is also paired and works with the solar plexus, you may want to take this into consideration as well.

Chapter 9

Invocations and Affirmations

When one runs with the wolves, one must howl with the pack
– Leon Trotsky

These invocations and affirmations are for you to use in ritual or sacred time and place when you wish to connect with or embody Wolf. They can be part of your daily practice or part of a special occasion or ceremony.

The **affirmations** can be inspirational and motivational or bring focus to that which you wish to achieve or manifest. They are designed to be affirmed and repeated as positive statements, with the intention of creating empowering thought patterns in your being. You can choose one a week and add it to your diary or calendar, pop one on a post-it on your mirror or fridge, or have it as the background on your phone. Every time you see it, repeat, affirm it, know it, be it.

The **invocations** you could use like a prayer or as ceremonial speech. Speak them out loud in ritual, record yourself saying one and listen as you sleep, or use them as a meditation to bring focus and alignment with that which you wish to manifest or embody. Words are sacred and they are magic; they create, they bring into being, so whichever way you choose to use them, do so with presence, loving intention and respect.

I have also recorded two of the invocations for you to join me in speaking them aloud in a ritual space. You can find these on my website.

AFFIRMATIONS

1. Like wolf I am courageous and I show up for that which needs me to be brave.
2. I remember that I am here on purpose, with a responsibility to myself and the world to be me, fully and completely.
3. My worth/value is determined by no one other than myself.
4. I persevere, because I know that I am capable and have something of value to offer.
5. I know my boundaries and I honour and maintain them with loving intention.
6. I am fiercely protected by my wolf guides and guardians.
7. I am deserving of a pack that will value me and treat me well.
8. My voice is my sacred vehicle for howling the songs of my heart and soul.
9. I express myself clearly and truthfully, with no shame or embarrassment.
10. I choose integrity and honour truth, harmony and justice.
11. I speak up for those that are vulnerable and contribute my spirit and fire to equality and opportunity for all.

INVOCATIONS

Grand Father Wolf Invocation, for Wisdom

You may want to use this invocation for a particular question, or any time that you feel you want to connect or listen to your inner, or divine, wisdom for advice, guidance or clarity. You can address this to any of the Grand Father Wolf deities, a particular guide, this aspect of yourself or just to the essence of Grand Father Wolf.

I open sacred space now to listen deeply with you, Grand Father Wolf.
I open my being to the great below, the great above and the great within.

I am still so that I may move into full potentiality,
I watch so that I may see all that is beyond sight,
I seek reflection so that I may journey into what I cannot understand.
I willingly enter the cave of dreams so that I may dream my soul awake.

Grand Father Wolf I ask for your support and guidance in listening to my intuition.
I ask now that I receive insight and revelation.
Bless my eyes, my ears, my inner knowing and heart,
May they be without judgement or conditions,
As I offer my questions, thoughts and worries.
May they be the sacred keys to open the door to deeper knowing.

I honour my inner wisdom, as both cosmic and divine.
I listen with respect and honour to both my wolf guides and my inner knowing.

I am listening.
I listen.

(Follow this invocation with time in silence, meditating, dreaming, sleeping, contemplating, automatic writing, drawing or asking specific questions or using oracle cards. When you feel you have completed this session, give thanks to Grand Father Wolf and your highest self.)

Invocation for warrior/warrioress courage

This invocation is for any time you want to call on the ferocious wolf aspect of yourself, or you want to embody courage or stand in your personal power.

I call forth the strength of my inner wolf.
And I call forth the strength of Wolf essence.

I choose now to call forth this strength,
So, I may have the courage to stand in my personal power.
I know and trust there is great strength within me, that is true and holy.
And I step forward to embody it now.

I press my mighty paws deep into the ground,
So that I may stand strong and aligned with my truth.
My experiences are what motivates me to share, to create, to pioneer change,
To offer myself in service and devotion,
To the earth, to peace, to life, to the pack of humanity.

This hunt through life has been my training programme.
I have journeyed through the cave into the depths of my shadow,
And now stand bravely in my authenticity,
Honest and true, whole and holy.
Who I am, is what I have to offer.
I will be warrior for all that my heart holds dear,
I will fight courageously for the earth and all that lives upon it.
I will let my voice howl with wisdom and truth.

I am not afraid.
I know that I follow in the footsteps of my ancestors,
And I have my Wolf guardians and allies beside me.

Armed with my wolf instinct, tenacity and their divine guardianship.
I make a stand,
I make a choice to be a warrior against greed, power-over, corruption and violence.

I am
She/ He / They who knows my own power,
She / He/ They who sits in service to the pack,
She / He/ They who values unity over divisiveness,
and stands for justice and equality.

With my wolf family, guides and guardians as my witness,
And through these sacred words,
I release beliefs keeping me small, scared and doubtful.
I release all that prevents me from standing in my power
from embodying my truth,
from embodying harmony,
from embodying courage,
from embodying love.

I am the integration of shadow and light,
I am powerful and gentle,
I am mighty and kind.
I am strong,
I am fierce,
I am bold,
I am a guardian of truth,
I am the essence of wolf.

And so I AM (3 times)
And so it is (3 times)
Blessed be (3 times)

Invocation for self-trust and belonging

This invocation is for anytime that you are feeling lost, doubtful, indecisive or for those lone wolves that desire to affirm that they belong, that they matter, that they have a place. For this invocation I invite you to have your bare feet on the earth or in shallow water, or sit below a tree or out in nature.

I am wolf.
I feel the elements, beneath me, around me, supporting me, holding me.
Always.
And I, with great courage, offer myself today the gift of presence.
Today, I choose to open my heart to strengthen my sense of belonging.

I honour what I have, who I am and where I am,
Exactly as I am.
I AM enough and there is nothing wrong with me or where I be.
I affirm that I belong here in my body.
(Place your hands upon your body)
And deep in the darkness of my womb/centre,
I plant a seed now.
A seed of trust,
A seed of hope,
A seed of reclamation of self.

I honour that it is time to grow and cultivate trust within me,
And I vow to nurture it with compassion and understanding.
I will give myself time, patience and honour my process.

I am wolf.
I trust that beneath my warm, wolf skin is a body that is my guide.

My body is my home,
It is my den,
That I must return to again and again.
Any time that I feel lost or doubtful I come home to my body.
I listen to my heart and remember that it beats for me,
I feel my body and remember it has been there every step, every stumble, every tear, every laugh, every moment of pleasure.
(Take a deep breath here, with your hands still upon your body)
I breathe deeply and feel my body sink, relax and surrender,
Into the loving arms of Mother Earth,
She that gave me this sacred breath.
I know that I am accepted and cared for, always.

Grounded and connected,
On this holy earth and in this sacred body of mine,
I claim my right to be acknowledged, loved, held, honoured and respected.
I am a blessing to myself and others.

I claim my value back from all the places it has been taken or dismissed.
I choose me.
I choose myself, as a statement and declaration, that I am worthy, I am valuable and I am important.
No one can judge me otherwise.
I call on my wolf guides and guardians to affirm this with me.
To bless my body,
to bless my heart,
to bless my dreams and wishes.
And to remind me daily that I am never lost, never abandoned, never alone,
Because my body is here, it is mine, it IS home.

Because the earth on which I sit/stand is my compass, my guide, my map.

I am . . . (and say your name)
And I belong here
I belong x3

Blessed be, Blessed me, Blessed we.

Invocation or Prayer to your Elemental Wolf

Use this invocation when you wish to work with or call upon your particular elemental wolf, or any of the elemental wolves. This invocation is designed to mark the beginning of any healing work, journaling, meditation or activity you wish to do. Add the element of your choice as appropriate. You can call upon more than one at a time if you wish.

(Place your hands upon your body and begin with saying)

I am here, I am present, I am me.
And I open sacred space now.
Anything that is not mine, that does not belong to me or serve my highest purpose I ask now to return to source with love and compassion.

(Take a deep breath and breathe out through your mouth)

I call on the element of . . . . *(add your element/s)*
And the Elemental Wolf Guardians of . . . . *(add your element/s)*
For the highest possible alchemical healing and transmutation that is possible today.
I acknowledge this element is within me and within you, my guides, and I hold it as sacred and holy.
I honour this element as a point of connection between me and the universe and the cosmos.
That which is within is without, what is without, is within.
The universe that brought into being all that I am and can be, I thank you and open to all that is possible now.

I honour the element of . . . *(insert your element/s)* and the ways in which it manifests within me.
And I ask that today through this sacred time and place,

That I learn how to . . .
(choose your element from the options below)
(For Ether) – hold and create space with the divine within and without. May I come into oneness, dissolving any points of separation or disconnection from all that is holy and sacred.
(For Air) – offer myself freedom and expansion into all that is possible. May I learn to inhale and exhale life with trust and surrender, and express my truth with clarity and honesty.
(For Fire) – tend to my inner flame and step into the flames of transformation and transfiguration with trust and courage.
(For Water) – embrace fluidity and flow. May the holy waters flow through my body and being now, moving all that is ready to be released, cleansed or purified.
(For Earth) –come into deeper connection with my body, as, from and of the earth. I explore how I can come into rooted and connected awareness, so I may be deeply nourished and grow authentically.

I ask for the guidance of the elements to reveal all that I am and all that I can be.
I ask that I come fully into alignment with all the ways in which I can receive and create,
And all the ways in which I can heal and be healed.
Elemental Wolf support me in seeing, listening, knowing, speaking and being all that you embody and advocate.
I honour, you, I thank you. I am ready.
And so it is (x3)
And so it will be (x3)

Mother Wolf invocation

This invocation is to connect with the energy and essence of Mother Wolf. She who is creatrix, birth keeper and fierce protector. You can also use this invocation if you wish to embody Mother Wolf and access the aspects of you that have the potential to, or need, nurturing and nourishing. This, like all the invocations, is for all genders, anyone can embody or connect to the mother archetype within.

Great Mother Wolf,
I call on you to be present here with me now.
Hear my longing for the abundance of your love,
And honour me with your steady and knowing energy.
I surrender into your warm and protective embrace,
Take me into your den so I may remember and affirm that I am love, loved and loving.

Within the great and holy womb of your being,
Support me in finding ease with my deepest wishes and needs.
Wrap your great paws around me so that I may feel safe and protected.
Guide me,
In receiving that which nourishes and awakens my potentiality,
And as I tend to my hopes and desires like they are my pups;
with care, compassion and encouragement.

Mother I hear your gentle whimpers that tell me to honour the desire within me,
The desire that longs to create and to nourish.
Help me softly surrender into tenderness and trust,
To accept your encouragement,
To release any shame or anxiety that I have around my abilities and capability.

To see and find the strength and power that lies in kindness and gentleness.

I release all pressures, expectations and limitations I have placed upon myself,
As woman, as feminine, as carer, as enabler, as creator, as protector, as human.
I let go of the striving for perfection and all of the 'shoulds' that keep me exhausted,
And all the ways that I have placed limiting conditions on receiving.
I release all of this now into your mighty wolf jaws to be transformed and transmuted into new ways of being.

You teach me that I am whole and holy, sacred and sovereign,
And knowing this,
I choose now to affirm that I am strong and capable.
I will love myself, just as you love me,
Love myself,
As a beautiful reflection of the divine feminine that creates and nurtures.
And that I ask for continued support for when I need to speak up for what is aligned and truthful for me.

I willingly and gratefully receive your motherhood and guidance, now and forever.
Thank you, I honour you, I love you.
And so, it is and so it will be.

Throat chakra clearing prayer

First ground yourself. You may want to be in a place that feels safe, where you can speak loud and clear and or make noises if you wish. Breath deep and imagine a blue light surrounding you. You may want to have your arms spread open, or your hands on your heart, throat or shoulders. You may also find that you want or need to move, please honour that in any way it manifests.

I call on my wolf guardians and guides to hold scared and safe pace for me now.
Surround me with your protection and support please.
(Take 3 deep breaths)

I am howling wolf.
I howl now for all that I did not express past, present and future.
I speak now for all that I wished I had said,
I speak now for all that I could not say,
Or would not say.
For all of the times it did not feel safe to speak, or ask,
For all of the unspoken yeses and no's,
For any times I felt shut down, my voice bound, condemned or unacknowledged.
I howl now and I release from my throat any stuck energy, words, thoughts or wounds,
That hold me back from expressing myself, my heart and my soul.
I release, I release, I release!
(You may want to howl, cry, shout, speak of any words that come forth, sing, make noise)

I am the wolf of whimpers,

I acknowledge that my words have the power to bring joy, to soothe, to bring pleasure and peace.
I can choose words of love!
There is always a choice.
And I choose now, love and truth.
I trust my heart to lead me in my expression.
May my voice and words be a bridge, a catalyst and a vehicle for kindness, compassion, encouragement and celebration.
(You may want to whimper, cry, whisper any words that come forth, sing, make soothing noise)

I am the wolf that growls,
I know that I am powerful!
I also see that my words can destroy and they create, they attract and they dispel.
And so, I call on the wisdom of my highest self and my guides,
I call forth the wisdom of the deepest parts of me and the cosmos.
So that I may speak henceforth with clarity, insight, awareness and consideration.
I courageously speak with honesty,
I create magic with every word,
And I take responsibility for that.
(You may want to growl, cry, bark, speak of any words that come forth, sing, make noise)

My voice is a point of connection,
My voice is a sacred vessel,
a sacred offering,
A sacred medium for cocreation and holy communion.
I acknowledge my power,
I acknowledge my voice.
I acknowledge the voice within and without and bring their polarity together in sacred union,

Communion,
So that my truth is always aligned with what I say, do and act.
I acknowledge the difference that I can be in the world,
And I speak in honour of that within me and on behalf of those that have no voice.
May my voice, expression and communication be a rising acapella for love and freedom.
And so it is and so it will be.

(You may want to howl again here, or offer any other further words, songs, noises of clearing, celebration or affirmation.)

Conclusions and Author's Note

The wolves knew when it was time to stop looking for what they'd lost, to focus instead on what was yet to come.
– Jodi Picoult

One of my first encounters with wolf essence was watching the *Jungle Book* as a child. I remember being captivated that Mowgli was rescued and brought up by the wolves and hoped the same would happen to me! It struck a chord so deep that throughout all the times in my life when I felt the outsider or that I didn't belong, I always knew that nature accepted me, loved me and held out her open arms. Wolves have given me the validation that I was essentially all that I needed to be and most definitely *not* wrong. They gave me a nudge to continue when I was labelled the odd one because I felt more at home dancing in the trees, than in school. They inspired courage when I was told how foolish I was for pursuing a career that made me happy and fulfilled, but wasn't quite the normal or expected route. The example and essence of wolves was a prominent ally when I sought and then gave myself permission to speak and be who I knew I was, rather than whom I was told I should be.

Mother Nature, of whom wolves are an essential component, never ceases to amaze me in how she gives again and again. She not only gives materially, but spiritually and emotionally. She provides for us, has provided for us, since the beginning of time and asks for nothing in return apart from that we respect her, love her and treat her well. She gives you the food you eat, the air you breath, your home, the clothes on your back, the water you drink, everything essential to your being alive is from her. Not only this but she inspires and motivates us, supplies the stardust for our dreams and offers us the opportunity and location to manifest those dreams. She is encouraging and accepting of all and sees us, loves us exactly as we are.

Writing this book feels to me a way of giving back to Wolf and Mother Earth. It is rooted in my gratitude and love. By facilitating this pathway and opportunity for you to also commune with her in a reverent way, this is my way of saying thank you. I am also here to support your deepening connection and appreciation of wolves, because when we learn to fully appreciate something and connect deeply to it, we come to value it. When we value something, we then care enough to protect it, to fight for it, to make a stand for its survival and maintenance.

Earth is your home and mother and wolves are your brothers and sisters. As we finish this journey together, I hope you now know this so deeply in your bones and heart that you are filled with a renewed regard and appreciation for your pack and den, as well as a deeper understanding of your important and irreplaceable place in both.

> *For the strength of the pack is the wolf, and the strength of the wolf is the pack.* — Rudyard Kipling

This book has highlighted the various opinions and viewpoints of wolves throughout time; sometimes sacred being and muse, sometimes a nuisance or nemesis that interferes with humanity's self-centred ultimatum. Both perspectives offer us insight into not just our viewpoints on Wolf but also on life and the fears, loves, passions and struggles of being human. I hope this book has ultimately shown you the immense healing and wisdom wolves offer, in both their example and from their essence, mythology and energy.

So, what can you now offer back after witnessing, reading and learning about their mighty and ferocious generosity?

You can choose to care about them and you can value them enough to make a positive and impactful difference in this world for and on behalf of nature. The persecution of wolves is still ongoing and the wolves need your help to survive. Hunting is still a practice; and the hunting of wolves still happens all over the world. It is not necessary, nor is it humane. And for those that argue that wolves kill prey and attack sheep, please look at the numbers of animals we kill daily on this planet, just for food, that is in consumption way more than we need and is most often wasted. We humans have been granted choice, free will and we have the sacred choice to decide whether we destroy or create and so this is our gift and our responsibility.

The reason wild wolves are hardly ever seen is because we humans are intimidating, they avoid us because we are the danger. They are naturally shy and cautious creatures. Yes, they have sometimes crossed over boundaries into human land, but in necessity because we have destroyed their natural habitat and over monopolised, even extinguished their natural prey and habitat. There is no reason why we cannot cohabit the earth that we share, with consideration, compassion and peace. The only barrier is human greed and arrogance.

Statistically we are the worst and most dangerous predator on this planet and there is a lot of destruction and death to be responsible for, to apologise for, to make up for. Around the year 1760 wolves became instinct in Britain, perhaps before the 300th anniversary we will see their reintroduction, I dearly hope so. I hope that their land is restored sustainably and then protected. I hope that humans can learn to open and find space in their hearts and minds for that which is made 'other' or different. I hope we can learn to face our fears with grounded and centred courage so that they can be transmuted into acceptance, understanding and tolerance.

Just as wolves guard us, let us also guard them. My worst fear is that one day we will only be able to connect with wolf spirit because there will be no living and breathing wolves left! Yet there is hope. I believe wolves are rising again in the consciousness now because they are asking for our help and want to re-establish that long and deep connection with us that goes way back to our very beginnings. We have created so much destruction, it is time for more collaboration, communion and cocreation rather than domination.

I wish the same liberation and empowerment for you as well. I pray that your wild, untamed wonderful self knows freedom from binds and captivity and that the parts of you that were made wrong, bad and ugly are given recognition and celebration by yourself and the world, so that are able you to shine in your unique and powerful frequency.

If we can learn to live with and integrate the wolf within, then we can begin learning to live with the real-life wolf in society and community. When we are led by fear, of self or others, our perspective is distorted, we see through only the tiny lense that fear creates, that blocks us from seeing possibility and change.

When we take steps to integrate both our shadow and our light, to embrace all of ourselves, without judgement or limiting conditions, so we can then offer this for others.

Let us have allowance for paradox and bring together that which has been made polar

In my own heart's version of Red Riding Hood, it is the guide and guardian of this book, Grand Mother Wolf, that Red visits in the dark forest. In her own journey, at what seems the darkest and hopeless place from which she cannot return, Grand Mother shows her how her eyes can see truth through illusion and mist ('The better to see you with'), how her ears can listen to her intuition ('the better to hear you with'), what she is hungry for, what her heart and souls desires ('the better to eat you with') and what she is truly capable of creating ('the better to grab you with'). Her time with the wolf is an initiation so she may emerge more whole than before, with a greater understanding of self and all her facets. Grand Mother Wolf's house truly is the womb-tomb of transformation, she will devour that which no longer supports you, nurture you while you incubate, guard you while you reclaim the wild parts of yourself and then send you out of the forest, back to live a life full of aligned purpose and fulfilment.

I hope you have enjoyed your time in the forest with Wolf and I send you forth with love and hope that your journey with Wolf continues to be both healing and empowering!

Sending so many blessings,

Rachel xx

Further Resources

Grand Mother Wolf is the ally that came forth to facilitate this book and she is the most ancient matriarch of the wolf essence. I have shared much of her wisdom in this book and she will further support you remembering the intimate and co-creative relationship between humankind and wolf.

To experience a free guided meditation with her as well as other wolf guides, such as Mars and Lupa, please visit my website www.wolfwomanrising.com

There are also many associations and charities that are doing such important work, in the back of this book I have included some wolf associations and charities that you can support, who in turn support the wolf population. The sharing of my work and this book, would also be an invaluable aid in the exposure of the great healing and wisdom of Wolf essence. So, share far and wide about Wolf and I would love to hear your experiences and reflections on social media.

Find me at:
Instagram www.instagram.com/wolfwomanrisingofficial
Youtube www.youtube.com@wolfwomanrising
Facebook www.facebook.com/wolfwomanrising and in our Facebook community group.

Keep in touch! You are also warmly invited to join me in further courses with Wolf to deepen your understanding and embodiment of the wolf within!

All of the resources I have mentioned throughout this book are available to you on my website. All are completely free and there to support the deepening of your journey with wolf! They include:

- Wolf Archetype Quiz
- Guided Audio Journey with Grand Mother Wolf
- Guided Audio Invocation ceremonies, using two invocations from this book
- An audio telling of Fenrir's story
- Specific altar decoration and ritual tools for each wolf deity

Visit www.wolfwomanrising/wolf

Links to Wolf Support

There are many associations and charities that are doing such important work for the earth and for wolves. Here I have included just some wolf associations and charities that you can support, who in turn support the wolf population.

If you know more and you would love for me to share their details or pages just let me know, or send me the link!

- The **North American** Wolf Education and Research Centre. https://www.wolfcenter.org/
- The International Wolf Centre https://wolf.org
- www.wwf.org.uk WWF is the world's leading independent conservation organisation.**UK Based**.
- Euronatur, **European** Nature Conservation – Germany https://www.euronatur.org
- Wolves in Saxony, **Germany** https://www.nlwkn.niedersachsen.de
- Nature and Biodiversity Conservation Union, is one of the oldest and largest environment associations in **Germany**. https://en.nabu.de/
- Skandulv – The Scandinavian Wolf Project – provides current news and population information regarding the wolves in **Scandinavia** http://skandulv.nina.no/english/Home.aspx
- **UK** Wolf Conservation Trust https://ukwct.org.uk/
- Wolves in **Romania** https://milvus.ro/Hu/mammals/10597-2/
- Return of the Wolf project is working promote wolf conservation in the **Italian** Alpine Arc region and support human-wildlife coexistence. https://rewildingeurope.com/rew-project/return-of-the-wolf-to-the-eastern-alps/
- **European** Alliance for Wolf Conservation (EAWC), a

coalition of NGOs advocating for the use of preventive non-lethal means to achieve coexistence with wolves, https://wolf-alliance.org/

- A movement to support the re-introduce of wolves and sustainable wolf and human cohabitation https://www.wolvesandhumans.org/conservation-of-wolves-in-europe

Endnotes

1 https://davemech.org/
2 p.7 *Wolves* by edit. D Mech
3 p.11 *The Jungle Book*
4 p..290 *Wolves*, edit by D. Mech
5 p..212 *Heraldry. Sources, Symbols and Meaning*
6 Find out more in my book *Lupa. She Wolf of Rome, Mother of Destiny*
7 p.45 *Animals in Celtic Life and Myth*
8 p.226 *The Living Goddess*
9 Find out more about Lupercalia and how to celebrate this wolf festival in my book *Lupa*
10 Find out more in my book *Lupa. She Wolf of Rome, Mother of Destiny*
11 See *The Wolf Within* by B. Sykes for an in depth look at research into biological heritage of wolves
12 https://www.nationalgeographic.com/science/article/neanderthals-caves-rings-building-france-archaeology
13 David Macdonald, taking about the origin of the Grey Wolf in *'The Velvet Claw. A Natural History of the Carnivores'*
14 Picture of Isis with Wolf. https://www.bmimages.com/preview.asp?image=00312895001
15 p.65 *Gods and myths of Northern Europe*
16 See my book *Lupa, She Wolf of Rome, Mother of Destiny*
17 Recipes kindly supplied by Talya Lutzker CEO, Ayurveda Every Day with Talya – Certified Ayurvedic Practitioner, Health and Lifestyle Expert, Author, Yoga Teacher http://www.ayurvedaed.com Thank you dear Talya!

Bibliography

Billington, Sandra & Green, Miranda (eds.), *The concept of the Goddess*. (London, Routledge, 1999).

Ellis Davidson, H. R., *Gods and Myths of Northern Europe*. (Middlesex, Penguin Books Ltd., 1964).

Green, Miranda., *Celtic Goddesses*. (London, British Museum Press, 1995).

Gimbutas, Marija., *The Living Goddess*. (London, University of California Press, 1999).

Kerven, Rosalind., *Viking Myths and Sagas. Retold from ancient Norse texts*. (Morpeth, Talking Stone, 2015).

Kipling, Rudyard., *The Jungle Books*. (Richmond. Alma Classics Ltd., 1894/ 2016?).

Leeming, David., *From Olympus to Camelot. The World of European Mythology*. (New York, Oxford University Press, 2003).

Livy, B.O. Foster (trans.) *The History of Rome. Volumes 1-2*. (London Heinemann, 1919).

MacCulloch, J. A., *The Celtic and Scandinavian Religions*. (London, Constable and Company Limited, 1994).

Macdonald, David., *The Velvet Claw. A natural history of the carnivores*. (London, BBC Books, 1992).

Merivale, Patricia., *Pan the Goat-God. His Myth in Modern Times*. (Oxford, Oxford University Press, 1969).

London Mech, L. David., *Wolves: behaviour, ecology and conservation*. (Chicago, University of Chicago Press, 2006).

Neubecker, Ottfried., *Heraldry. Sources, Symbols and Meaning*. (London, MacDonald and Co Publishers, 1988).

Ovid., *Metamorphoses*. Mary. M. Innes (ed. And trans.) (London, Penguin Books, 1955).

Roxburgh, D. J. (ed.) *Turks, A Journey of a Thousand Years*. (London, Royal Academy of Arts, 2005).

Suziiedelis, Saulius A., *Historical Dictionary of Lithuania.* (Lanham, Scarecrow Press, 2011).

Sykes, Bryan., *The Wolf Within, The Astonishing Evolution of Man's Best Friend.* (London, William Collins Books, 2019).

Online

Kaczensky P., Chapron G., von Arx M., Huber D., Andrén H. & Linnell, J. (Eds.) 2013. *Status, management and distribution of large carnivores – bear, lynx, wolf & wolverine – in Europe. Part I.* Europe summaries. A large Carnivore Initiative for Europe Report prepared for the European Commission.

ŠKVOR JERNEJČIČ, Brina ; TOŠKAN, Borut. Ritual use of dogs and wolves in the Late Bronze and Early Iron Age in the South-Eastern Alpine region. New evidence from the archaeo(zoo)logical perspective in: *Animal symbolisé, animal exploité: du Paléolithique à la Protohistoire* [online]. Paris: Éditions du Comité des travaux historiques et scientifiques, 2018 (generated 25 janvier 2023).

About the Author

For those of you that may be interested in my background!

I am a glittery and very fluffy variety of wolf that lives and roams in North Wales, U.K. I read History with Religious Studies (BA Honours) at university and then went on to complete post-graduate qualifications in History and Heritage Management. I have also worked in the heritage sector for over a decade, primarily working with children, learning and interpretation and I can claim to have worked in five different castles!

My desire has always been to create a bridge between history and spirituality, to offer historic knowledge as a holistic tool, transmuting mythology into embodied wisdoms, so that is becomes a bridge to healing, empowerment and awakening for men and women.

And so, running parallel to my love of history, I am also a sacred dance teacher, priestess, empowerment coach and flower essence practitioner. I have been teaching since 2006.

In my role as priestess and leader, I facilitate and lead the **Wolf Woman Rising Wisdom School** that brings together ancient mythology and history with embodiment tools and practices, such as meditation, sacred dance and nature alchemy. I support students in actualising courage and authenticity and bringing forth their soul's truth and destiny to be the difference they wish to see and create.

As well as Wolf Woman Rising, I am also the founder and principal teacher of **Under the Dancing Tree School of Sacred Dance**. I teach sacred dances including Belly Dance, Polynesian dance, movement meditation and facilitate various mediums of healing dance.

Using my own journey and nearly two decades of experience in teaching and training I infuse spirituality and the divine into my dance and teachings. I do so to empower, and inspire students to live their most aligned and purposeful life and to explore dance as a powerful means to express emotion and facilitate healing of mind, body, soul and heart.

Encompassing all of this I offer online community, courses and training, as well as in-person retreats and workshops.

Find out more:
For my wisdom school of wild embodiment
www.wolfwomanrising.com
For sacred dance and movement healing:
www.underthedancingtree.co.uk
Or connect with me @wolfwomanrising

You may also like

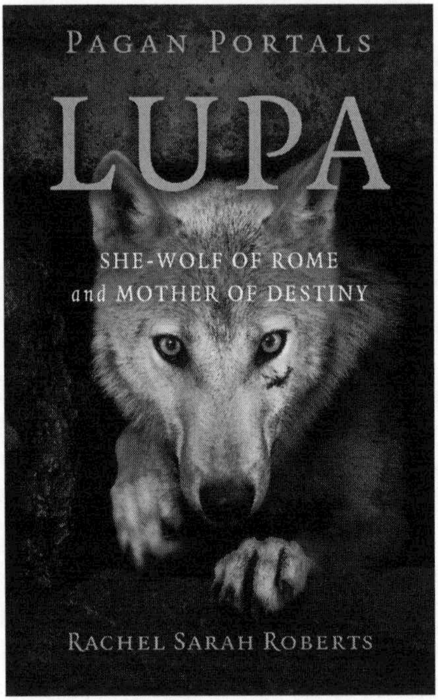

Lupa Cover

Pagan Portals – Lupa
She-Wolf of Rome and Mother of Destiny

Explore the mythos of Lupa and its meaning and importance for the Ancient Romans – as well as for you now

978-1-80341-350-1 (Paperback)
978-1-80341-351-8 (e-book)

MOON BOOKS

PAGANISM & SHAMANISM

What is Paganism? A religion, a spirituality, an alternative belief system, nature worship? You can fi nd support for all these definitions (and many more) in dictionaries, encyclopaedias, and text books of religion, but subscribe to any one and the truth will evade you. Above all Paganism is a creative pursuit, an encounter with reality, an exploration of meaning and an expression of the soul. Druids, Heathens, Wiccans and others, all contribute their insights and literary riches to the Pagan tradition. Moon Books invites you to begin or to deepen your own encounter, right here, right now.

If you have enjoyed this book, why not tell other readers by posting a review on your preferred book site.

Bestsellers from Moon Books

Keeping Her Keys

An Introduction to Hekate's Modern Witchcraft

Cyndi Brannen

Blending Hekate, witchcraft and personal development together to create a powerful new magickal perspective.

Paperback: 978-1-78904-075-3 ebook 978-1-78904-076-0

Journey to the Dark Goddess

How to Return to Your Soul

Jane Meredith

Discover the powerful secrets of the Dark Goddess and transform your depression, grief and pain into healing and integration.

Paperback: 978-1-84694-677-6 ebook: 978-1-78099-223-5

Shamanic Reiki

Expanded Ways of Working with Universal Life Force Energy

Llyn Roberts, Robert Levy

Shamanism and Reiki are each powerful ways of healing; together, their power multiplies. Shamanic Reiki introduces techniques to help healers and Reiki practitioners tap ancient healing wisdom.

Paperback: 978-1-84694-037-8 ebook: 978-1-84694-650-9

Southern Cunning

Folkloric Witchcraft in the American South

Aaron Oberon

Modern witchcraft with a Southern flair, this book is a journey through the folklore of the American South and a look at the power these stories hold for modern witches.

Paperback: 978-1-78904-196-5 ebook: 978-1-78904-197-2

Bestsellers from Moon Books
Pagan Portals Series

The Morrigan
Meeting the Great Queens
Morgan Daimler
Ancient and enigmatic, the Morrigan reaches out to us. On shadowed wings and in raven's call, meet the ancient Irish goddess of war, battle, prophecy, death, sovereignty, and magic.
Paperback: 978-1-78279-833-0 ebook: 978-1-78279-834-7

The Awen Alone
Walking the Path of the Solitary Druid
Joanna van der Hoeven
An introductory guide for the solitary Druid, The Awen Alone will accompany you as you explore, and seek out your own place within the natural world.
Paperback: 978-1-78279-547-6 ebook: 978-1-78279-546-9

Moon Magic
Rachel Patterson
An introduction to working with the phases of the Moon, what they are and how to live in harmony with the lunar year and to utilise all the magical powers it provides.
Paperback: 978-1-78279-281-9 ebook: 978-1-78279-282-6

Hekate
A Devotional
Vivienne Moss
Hekate, Queen of Witches and the Shadow-Lands, haunts the pages of this devotional bringing magic and enchantment into your lives.
Paperback: 978-1-78535-161-7 ebook: 978-1-78535-162-4